MW01280144

"FOR YOU THE WAR IS OVER"

A FLYBOY'S EXPERIENCE OF

WORLD WAR II

CARL WELLER

Carl Weller

edited by Jeff Duncan

To Al Chase and Henry Benitez

my B-17 crew mates who
didn't make it

(with special thanks to Wendy and Barb)

CONTENTS

Preface

For years friends, children, and family have asked me to tell them about my experiences from WWII. Like most WWII vets I knew, I was not able to talk about it. But then fifteen years ago, while sitting in a Honolulu coffee shop with my daughter, much to her surprise, and mine, I started talking. Memories came flooding back.

After that I tried to write down my feelings, thoughts, history. I would stare at a blank page unable to form a time line or a way to make sense of it.

Then last year, when Jeff Duncan encouraged me to take up that journey with him, it seemed like there was now going to be a way to put it down on paper. Jeff's easy, kind, and down-to-earth manner helped me see the story of my own life. One memory led to another, and long-forgotten memories began to surface. His patience was extraordinary. I am so grateful for the opportunity he gave me to accomplish this in my twilight years.

It is with heartfelt appreciation and love that I thank Jeff Duncan, his wife Barb, and my daughter Wendy.

Thank you, Jeff, from the bottom of my heart.

Carl Weller
Staff Sergeant
8th Air Force
379 Bomb Group

Foreword

I have known Carl Weller for many years, and I knew that he flew in a bomber in World War II, was shot down, got captured, and did time in a German prison camp. But that was all I knew, because, like so many WWII vets, he didn't talk about his time in the Service in any detail. Not to me anyway, or anyone else I knew or knew of. Too painful, I assumed. Better to let sleeping dogs lie, and if they weren't asleep exactly, they were at least fairly quiet and better not to stir them up. But then almost a year ago we were having dinner at a restaurant together and he started recounting some episodes of his time in the Air Corps, and then said he thought that maybe he should get his experience of the war down in a book.

Well, Carl is not a writer and I figured he probably never would write that book himself (I didn't know he had tried to some years before), so I offered to help him make one. I would record him telling his story, then edit it. I told him not to worry about chronology, just describe events as they occurred to him and I would put them in chronological order. When he didn't remember certain facts we could do a fact-check, and whatever I found I would run past him for verification. (One of the facts I found that he never mentioned—Carl is a very modest man—was that he was awarded the Distinguished Flying Cross.) I would also take care of the repetitions that are inevitable in telling a long story for two and three hours at a time over the course of several weeks, but I would never mess around with his voice—it would be *his* story in *his* words; it would be *his* experience of World War II as best he could remember.

I'm glad to say he agreed, and this book is the result. I must say, knowing Carl these many years has been one of the great pleasures of my life, and helping

him get his story down one of the great honors.

Jeff Duncan

PART 1 – GOING TO WAR

The day after Pearl Harbor I went to school (I was a senior at Southeastern High, in Detroit) and found that I was one of only two boys in my class. All the other boys, and just about every male in my neighborhood, it seemed, was trying to join up. That was the way it was—everybody was patriotic and all gung-ho to join the Service, get in the fight. I was embarrassed and felt guilty that I had *not* skipped school, because I wanted to join in the fight myself.

I wanted in the Air Corps because I was nuts about airplanes. We lived fairly near City Airport, and I used to walk over there to watch the planes take off and land. My favorite hobby was making model airplanes, by hand, the kind that you made out of balsa wood and tissue paper with a propeller in front and one in back that you wound up with rubber bands and turned loose. We called that free flight, and part of the fun was chasing after the plane to wherever it landed. I was always just fascinated by airplanes, so even though I had never been up in one, I felt the Air Corps was the place for me to go.

I tried to join up, but they wouldn't take me without a signed statement by my parents saying that it was okay by them even though I was only seventeen years old. But it was *not* okay by them—"No way," they said: "no way!"—so I decided to wait and get drafted after I turned eighteen.

But I still wanted to do something for the war effort, so I quit school and got a job at Bauer Roller

Bearing, a factory near where we lived. Working was nothing new to me. I got my first job when I was around twelve. Actually, my uncle got me the job, a runner for a bookie named Big Al. Big Al took bets on the horse races, and sure enough, his office was in the back room of a pool hall, with a door that was a one-way mirror—from inside you could see through it, but from outside you could only see your reflection. I picked up bets from folks in the neighborhood (and loads of people bet on the ponies, including my straight-laced mother)—I picked up bets, stuffed them into an envelope, and delivered them to Big Al's "office," and later I delivered payoffs to the lucky winners. It was the Depression, you know, and money was scarce, so you did anything you could to help out with household expenses and to have some money for yourself.

In high school I got a straight job, strictly legal, with a furniture store. I cleaned up the place, helped them with deliveries. Although it was a furniture store, it also had appliances, and radios—no TV then—and sometimes we delivered refrigerators and chests of drawers up several flights of stairs. It was pretty hard work.

Besides the furniture store I did little odd jobs when I got the chance. I remember one time when I walked past a nearby lumber yard and noticed some pieces of scrap lumber laying around, so I asked if I could pick them up, and they said yes, just be careful, there's a lot of machinery there, it could be dangerous. They set out certain times for me to come in and pick up the scrap lumber. I would break it up to size to use as firewood, tie bundles of it up with rope, and sell it to people.

4

Everybody had furnaces in those days. You could burn wood or coal, but whatever you burned, you had to start the fire by hand with wood. We didn't have automatic gas like we have today. So you'd have to put some papers in the furnace, and some wood on top, then start with that. Once the fire took, you put some coal or bigger pieces of wood in. It was quite a job, keeping the house warm. And most houses didn't have fans to blow the heat out and spread it around. It sort of just stayed put and hung around the furnace. So for heat we'd also use the oven in the kitchen. Often the second stories didn't have *any* heat. So I collected scraps of lumber for a little while, until someone complained about it. Said it was too dangerous, having a kid out there in the yard like that, so I was told I couldn't gather lumber any more.

But I had noticed they had a lot of sawdust there, big piles of it, so I thought maybe I could pick up sawdust and put it in a box or a bag and sell it to butcher shops. All the butcher shops in those days had sawdust on the floor, to hold down the dust and help keep the place, well, not clean exactly, but sanitary, in that the dust wouldn't get on the meat. I sold the sawdust to some of the butcher shops, and that worked for a little while, but then the butchers said the sawdust was too fine to hold down the dust, and that was the end of that little money-maker.

We never talked about it, but whenever I made any money, like say ten dollars, I would give my mother eight and keep two for myself. I always felt a responsibility for that, for the household. Because of the times we were going through. The Depression taught you a lot about money. The value of money. And of pitching in. Didn't even think about it—I just helped out automatically.

Even when I went into the Service, I would have twenty five-dollars taken out of my pay and sent to my family. About half of my salary when I was first in. My salary started going up a little bit, a raise when I got to be a corporal, another raise when I got to be a sergeant, another for staff sergeant. And when I went overseas and got on the active combat list, I started getting hazard pay to boot, ten percent of my gross. When we got shot down and put in prison camp, I was still being paid, but of course couldn't get the money there, so what I had designated for the family, which remained at fifty per-cent, kept going home and my cut just kept building up in the bank.

Anyway, I got a job at Bauer Roller Bearing because I had heard they made roller bearings for aircraft engines and things like that, so I could help out with the war effort. We lived in a pretty tough section of Detroit, and the factory was right close to my house, in walking distance. I worked there until I got my draft notice.

When I got my draft notice I was told to report to Camp Custer, which was north of Kalamazoo, in Michigan. Guys from all over the States were there, to get initiated into the service, to get their barracks bags for their stuff, to get their uniforms, to get used to Army protocol, to get their assignments. While getting outfitted and getting our assignments, they kept us busy cleaning the barracks, scrubbing the floors, scouring the latrines, maintaining the grounds, that kind of thing. It wasn't boot camp, but they were letting us know this *was* the army.

They made assignments to fit the men into the various needs of the army—infantry, artillery, armored, and so forth. I went to the guy who assigned everyone to the various branches, went to him again and again and again, talked about flying, and how I used to hang out at City Airport and make model airplanes, and how I really, really, really wanted to be in the Air Corps. I must have convinced him because that's where he put me. I think I just wore him down.

I was at Custer for almost two weeks. Normally you were there for just a few days, then sent off to boot camp, which could be anywhere—Texas, Nebraska, New Jersey, wherever. I was there for two weeks because they had to special order shoes that would fit me. I was only a ten and a half, but I had a narrow foot. They said they couldn't release me—they couldn't release anyone—until I had the complete uniform. They had to special order my shoes, which came from Boston or someplace like that. Get a load of that: custom shoes in the Army! That took two weeks. While I was waiting, they let me go home weekends, which was fine and dandy by me.

During those two weeks I was working on the grounds one day, trimming grass or something, and this sergeant told me, "Go get that truck and bring it over here."

I said, "I don't know how to drive."

He said, "What! What do you mean, you don't know how to drive? You're eighteen years old and you don't know how to drive?" It was like he was saying, "What kind of an American are you, anyway?"

I said, "Well, our family's never had a car. We've had to walk everywhere, or take the bus." Which was true. When I was a baby my father had been seriously injured in a coal mining accident in Pennsylvania; as a consequence, he couldn't drive, so he never bought a car and didn't teach any of his kids how to drive. Didn't have drivers-ed in those days. So we went everywhere by bus or by foot. We called going by foot the "shoe-leather express."

From Custer I was sent to boot camp in Atlantic City. This boot camp was very unusual, even odd. They put us in these big old swanky hotels that the army had taken over. They G.I.'d everything—cleared out all the furniture and art from the rooms, ripped up all the carpet, replaced the regular beds with bunk beds, turned the kitchens and dining rooms into mess halls—all the trappings of a barracks in the Army. They didn't want us to enjoy the comforts of a luxury hotel—we were preparing for war, after all.

They got us up early in the morning. Early! Crack of dawn or earlier. We'd line up for breakfast, and after breakfast we'd fall out into marching order. We'd march down to the beach, and there were instructors there for exercises, calisthenics, to toughen our bodies up. After calisthenics they'd teach us how to march, to walk in step, in cadence, make left turns, right turns, about faces. We'd march a few miles, then have lunch. After lunch there'd be more calisthenics and marching. After dinner there was guard duty, three or four hour shifts through the night. I have to say it felt silly, guarding an Atlantic City hotel and the boardwalk, but we had to do it.

One thing that was really great about having boot camp in Atlantic City: the mess hall had been a dining room that had a stage and a dance floor, and after dinner we had a swing band for an hour or so playing the hit songs of the day. The pop music in those days was all dance music—dancing was extremely popular back then, maybe the major form of entertainment: foxtrot, jitterbug, swing. But since we were all guys, not many of us danced. Once in a while a couple of guys would dance together, but very few. Women dance with each other all the time, but guys? Even today that's rare, and back then it was not only unusual—it was suspicious.

We also entertained ourselves when we had some time on our hands. We played cards, checkers, chess; we told stories, tall tales, and lies; we lagged quarters, where you toss a quarter at a line, as many guys as wanted to play, and whoever was closest got all the quarters. Then you'd lag again. It was a form of gambling, but with very little luck involved—some of the guys were really good.

We made up a game we really enjoyed. On every floor there was a Coke machine, and we saved our empties. Those were the greenish-colored six-ounce glass bottles that were so thick and heavy they were almost unbreakable. We would set up our empties like bowling pins, but instead of rolling a ball at them, we would roll an empty Coke bottle, which would go every whichaway. That added an element of chance and surprise and suspense. And fun too, including the racket the bottles made.

Being in Atlantic City, we did our marching up and down the boardwalk. We often sang marching songs at the same time, call-and-response songs to help us keep the cadence and our energy up. The drill sergeant would sing, "You had a good home but then you left," and we'd respond, "You're right!" Then he'd repeat it: "You had a good home but then you left," and we'd repeat, "You're right!" Then he'd sing, "Sound off!" and we'd sing, "One two!" He'd repeat, "Sound off," and we'd answer "Three four!" Then he'd sing, "Cadence count," and we'd sing, "One two thee four one two.....three-four!"

Every once in a while there were complaints from the townies and the tourists that we were singing too loud, that we should quiet down, but we didn't. Most of us were teenagers: singing loud was fun, and the louder the better.

Marching in formation on the boardwalk made for an unusual difficulty: when you got all these men, hundreds of them, stepping in unison, after a while the boardwalk would start rattling and swaying like a swing bridge. It felt like the walk might break. So they would say, "Route set!" and we would break stride for a while. *That* made us pipe down—you can't sing marching songs when you're not in step.

One Sunday, a beautiful day, another G.I and I decided to go down to the beach and go swimming. We got bathing suits from somewhere, I don't recall, and went in swimming for a while, then laid down on the beach and fell asleep. Both of us. By the time we woke up we were burned. Burned so badly they put us in the hospital for two days. (We didn't have sunscreen back then.) They smeared Vaseline all over us, as gently as they could but it still hurt like hell, then put a tent over each of us so the sheet wouldn't touch our bodies—that's how bad it was.

Basic training took about ninety days.

From Atlantic City I was sent to Lowry Field near Denver, Colorado, for gunnery school. I was okay with being a gunner. When I was a kid my dad went hunting with buddies for rabbits and pheasants, and I really wanted to go with them, but for several years they wouldn't let me. Said I was too young, too little. Finally they let me go along, but they didn't let me shoot. What they had me do was stomp around clumps of grass and bushes to flush out the game. Finally they gave me permission to shoot, but I had to buy my own gun.

There was this outdoors magazine that had a standing offer: sell so many subscriptions to the magazine and you got a .410 single-shot shotgun. Well, I sold the subscriptions, got the shotgun, and went hunting with my dad and his buddies. I liked it, a lot. I learned how to keep the gun in good working order—I always cleaned it right after every hunt, *and* my dad's: he just couldn't be bothered with maintenance. Very importantly, it turned out, I also learned how to lead a moving target. I was actually a good shot. So being a gunner suited me just fine.

At Lowry we had classes eight hours a day, six days a week, plus drills and drills and more drills. We started from scratch, by learning how to use various tools: wrenches, screwdrivers, pliers, and the like.

Sounds pretty basic, but they didn't want to take anything for granted. And there *were* guys, a few, who hardly knew a wrench from a hammer.

Then we started learning firearms, from small arms on up to fifty-caliber machine guns, the ones we would be using in combat. We had to know the names of every part of the machine gun, and we had to learn how to take it apart and put it back together again. Then we had to learn how to take it apart and put it back together again while wearing gloves. It gets cold at high altitudes, you know. *Then* we had to learn how to take it apart and put it back together again blind-folded. I'm not quite sure why. Maybe because with night flights you can't see what you're doing, but as I learned later, the Brits flew their missions at night and we flew ours during the day. I don't know: maybe it was *just in case* we flew at night. Finally, we had to disassemble and reassemble the gun with gloves on *and* blindfolded at the same time. That was quite a trick, but we learned to do it.

One thing I really *loved* about gunnery school, they had a skeet range, where you shot clay pigeons flying in midair. They gave you a shotgun and a box of shells, and you had a little stand to set them on. There were twenty-five shells per box, so if you hit twenty-five pigeons, you got a perfect score. We got to the point where we could hit twenty-five out of twenty-five every time. All of us.

Shooting skeet taught you how to lead a target, which, as I said, I already knew how to do, but a lot of guys were beginners. The rationale was that when you're firing at an airplane, you're shooting at a moving target, so naturally you have to know how to lead it. In combat it was even more complicated: you'd be shooting at an airplane that could be going at different angles, different speeds, different altitudes, but skeet was a logical way to get you started at shooting a moving target.

After we learned to shoot skeet we learned to shoot targets from the back of a moving truck. They'd put you on a course with a rifle, and as you went along, mechanical soldiers would pop up one at a time and you'd shoot at them. They appeared quite fast, and disappeared even faster. Good training for reflexes. So in skeet you were shooting a moving target from a stationary position, and with the trucks you were shooting at a stationary target from a moving position.

We also had films where it was like you were in an airplane, like a B-17, and you would be standing in your position, and the film would have planes flashing by for you to shoot at. All this was really good training, and since I already enjoyed shooting, this was all great fun for me.

We were in Lowry for ninety days, and from there we went to the Laredo Air Force Base in Laredo, Texas. Southern Texas. Hot and dry! At Laredo we learned how to shoot the fifty-caliber machine guns that we could now disassemble and reassemble in our sleep. And to shoot them with proficiency. We started by shooting at moving targets from a stationary platform, then we shot at stationary targets from a moving platform—the same progression as at Lowry.

The next step was a huge one. We went airborne, to learn how to shoot at a moving target from a moving platform. Up to that time I had never been on an airplane in my life. They put me on a small plane—it wasn't a piper cub, but it was like that—a small little plane that had a fifty-caliber machine gun attached to it, and it was a flexible gun, meaning you could turn it side to side, up and down. Then they had another plane

21

pulling a target, a sleeve, by a line that was several feet long. The bullets you used were dyed a certain color, say red. Every fifth or sixth one was dyed—these were machine guns with a lot of bullets, so they didn't color all of them. When the plane pulling the target came by you, you shot at the sleeve. When you hit the sleeve the colored bullet would leave its color on it, so it was easy to tally your score.

The only caution they gave us was pretty obvious: don't shoot the airplane pulling the sleeve.

Shooting from a moving plane at a moving target was a whole new ball game, much, much more difficult than what we'd done before. A B-17's cruising speed was like two hundred and sixty miles an hour, and a German fighter could come in at you at say three hundred miles an hour, so the closing speed between bomber and fighter could be like five hundred miles an hour! Hardly any time at all. I was a waist gunner, and we fired through a window in the side of the plane—a large window, but still with restricted vision, so we had an absolute max of three seconds to spot the sleeve, aim, and shoot. Very fast, very tricky. That speed in combat was what we were simulating in training.

Well, on this little plane the pilot had a seat to sit on, but the gunner stood on the floor of the plane, on a platform of sorts made out of wood, and he wore a harness with a cable on it that hooked to the floor so he couldn't fall out. Otherwise there was nothing around, not even windows because the plane was just open, sides and top. There was a passenger seat at one time, but they had taken it out because waist gunners didn't have seats—we had to stand. When the plane dropped you could feel yourself getting lifted up; when the plane lifted up you could feel yourself getting pushed down. I think the pilots were having fun, especially with guys like me, who'd never been on a plane before.

The pilot said to me, "Okay, when you see the targets, shoot. And when you're all done, just pat me on the top of my head and I'll take you down." So when I was done, I started to pat him on his head, but he was way ahead of me. He gunned the motor and banked into a radical turn and down we went. I hit that cable and thought I was going to fall out, but it held. Oh, that was a thrill, let me tell you.

We didn't just practice shooting at Laredo. We got instruction in hand-to-hand combat techniques, and in the use of hand weapons and survival kits in case we got downed in enemy territory and had to fight somebody one-on-one. We were thrown fully clothed into a swimming pool with a rubber raft to simulate ditching in the North Sea. They had machine guns set to shoot at a certain height over the ground, and they had barbed wire set out, so we had to learn to crawl infantry-style while keeping our asses down, under the barbed wire, under the bullets. Real bullets.

The rationale for this drill was knowing how to crawl in case you got shot down and wanted to move while laying low. I was disappointed and a little ticked off because I joined the Air Corps partly because there was no mud in the clouds, and there I was, crawling through it like a dogface. But I have to say, there was a lot of mud in Germany, I found that out. And as it turned out, toward the end of the war we were actually able to put this training to use, but in a way we didn't anticipate.

Training was hard and actually dangerous— people got hurt and even killed. Our pilot saw two B-17's collide in mid-air: one went straight down, killing everyone except the tail gunner, he said, who walked away from the wreckage. The other plane kept flying

somehow. And guys did get hit by bullets, though I

never saw that happen myself. Plus broken limbs, con-

cussions from head blows, accidental wounds—it was a

tough business.

When we were done in Laredo we went to the

Gene Autry Air Force Base in Ardmore, Oklahoma. One

of the things that really fascinated me there was the

Indians we'd see downtown, just hanging out on the

corners and looking around, with big ten-gallon hats on,

still as statues—they were totally fascinating to me, a boy

from Detroit who'd never seen Indians before. I knew it

was rude, but I couldn't help but stare.

Ardmore was a great training spot for flying

because it was near the Arbuckle Mountains (a big

surprise to me: my only image of Oklahoma was the

wind sweeping down the plains), and there were strong

updrafts and downdrafts to learn how to handle. Sort of like the turbulence we would run into in Europe.

It was in Ardmore that they formed us into crews. Once our crew was formed we started flying make-believe missions, to get the hang of flying together, working together. One time we were flying to Galveston, Texas, to get used to the kind of long flights we would be making in Europe, but in Galveston the wind was blowing so hard it made it super hard for us to land. The wind would blow us out of the path, and we didn't want to land on the side of the runway, in dirt, so the pilot would give her the gun and go back up, make another circle to line up for a landing, and try again. This happened several times. We finally did land, and we did get back to Gene Autry.

The basic point of this training was for the crew to develop into a team. The team thing was very important in a B-17, where we all had specific jobs to do, and we could be counted on to do them, to be able to rely on each other in case of trouble. Had to be a lot of trust. That flight to Galveston put us through a lot and helped us develop that teamwork.

We practiced bombing targets outlined to scale. We even practiced night bombing, even though Americans didn't do night bombing in Europe. Like I said, the British bombed at night. They thought it was safer, but they couldn't see to aim their bombs very well, and their bombs fell hit-or-miss, often missing the targets not just by a mile, but by several miles. But in a way the Brits didn't care, because they wanted to inflict as many casualties as possible, in retaliation for the Germans' blitz attacks on London, which killed thousands and thousands of people, and also in the hope that the German people would get demoralized and force Hitler to surrender.

They also figured the Germans could rebuild factories and bridges faster than they could replace people, so taking out people made sense.

The American idea was to bomb by day, so we could see and hit the targets better, more accurately, and with tight formations and sufficient fighter escort, the danger wasn't that much greater than night bombing. It did take quite a while to get enough fighter escort, though, especially on long missions, which didn't really happen until the P-51 Mustangs arrived on the scene—they were faster and had greater range than the other fighters—and in the meantime we suffered pretty heavy casualties. Anyway, we did practice some night bombing, "just in case," I guess—but with such poor visibility, we once hit an electrical substation and blew it up. What can you say?—accidents happen. Especially in the dark.

I should also say that toward the war's end, we were bombing entire cities like the Brits did, cities like Nuremburg, Hamburg, Dresden, Berlin, reducing them to rubble. As you can see from photos, they looked like hell with the roof blown off. Like the British, we were trying to get Hitler to come to his senses and give up before his whole country was in ruins, but he didn't. Crazy son of a bitch. It worked in Japan, though.

We practiced formation flying a lot. The formations were called javelins at first, because of the way the planes lined up, but later were called combat boxes. A combat box was made up of three squadrons of six airplanes, the squadrons formed into groups of three, each in a triangle. Triangles making triangles. One squad flew higher than the lead box, the third squad under the lead. From top to bottom was like a hundred and fifty feet. Then the squads formed into a group, three boxes of eighteen bombers each, and the groups formed into wings of fifty-four aircraft, and the wings into divisions. A mission could include up to like a thousand planes—bombers, that is—plus fighter planes. The vertical wedge of a wing could stretch three thousand feet top to bottom, and a large formation, the kind that would hit Berlin, could stretch three hundred miles from front to back.

The last plane in a formation was called Tail End Charlie, and the right rear corner of a formation was called Coffin Corner. You can tell by the names that neither was a position you wanted to be in. Add the escort fighter planes—on the great big missions, pushing a thousand—and the noise was deafening, not only to us, but to the folks down below, loud enough to make the earth shake, literally.

The purpose of the formation was to provide maximum defense for the bombers—from whatever angle a German fighter attacked the B-17's, the pilot had to pass through a crisscross of fire from dozens of fifty-caliber machine guns. The tighter the formation, the better off you were, so you had to keep your place, which wasn't easy because the turbulence from all the propellers of all those planes, and the explosions of the anti-aircraft shells, along with the normal turbulence of weather, made steering really tough. The pilots had to manhandle the controls to stay in control.

A formation also helped make sure that the planes didn't get in each other's way and run into each other, or shoot each other, which was a real danger with hundreds of planes flying together, many of them only a hundred feet apart.

We also practiced strafing, where you fly in low and shoot ground targets with the machine guns and rockets and small bombs. Not that B-17's did much strafing—that was a job for fighter pilots—but the idea was to train us for any and every contingency, I guess. For strafing targets we used large white panels stretched out on the ground. Well, a local lady called the base one day and complained that we were strafing the sheets on her clothesline. We could understand her upset, but still thought it was funny.

Like I said, in Ardmore we got crew assignments. A B-17 had a crew of ten. Up in the plexiglass nose of the plane was the bombardier and the navigator, and each of those guys had a fifty-caliber machine gun for when they weren't navigating or sighting the target. Our bombardier was Wiley Hansen and our navigator was Homer Gregory.

The bombardier had the Norden bombsight to work with, and it was an amazing piece of technology. Its precision was beyond anything the Germans or the Japanese had. It was so valuable that it wasn't part of the standard equipment on the plane. The bombardier had to check it out from the dispensary before a flight and install it in the plane, and after a mission was over he had to take it out of the plane and check it back in to the dispensary. Those bomb sights were under lock and key at all times that they weren't on the plane.

The navigator gave the pilot the information he needed to steer the ship. It was a very complicated, very technical job, using radio, the topography of the ground beneath (when he could see the ground beneath), even the stars when flying in the dark, as in the old, *old* days before there was all the technology he had at his disposal. He had to be really good at math and geometry to keep the plane on track to the destination and back home. And if you got hit and an engine or two were knocked out and you got separated from your formation, the navigator had to figure out how to get back, and if you couldn't get back, he'd have to figure out a course for a new destination.

When he wasn't navigating he had a gun, a single fifty-caliber that he could shoot through a little hole in the side of the ship.

Above and behind those guys was the pilot, Bob Felgar, and the co-pilot, Ralph Irwin. Needless to say, their job was to fly the plane.

Those guys—the pilot, copilot, navigator, and bombardier—were officers. Lieutenants. The rest of us—engineer, radio man, gunners—were sergeants.

Behind the pilots was Al Chase, our flight engineer. Engineer was a sort of jack-of-all-trades-handyman position for taking care of things gone wrong or going wrong—he knew just about everything about the plane there was to know. He didn't have a seat. He stood up. He would make sure the wheels were up after takeoff, and make sure they were down for landing. Sometimes the wheels wouldn't come down by themselves, but there was a crank in the bomb bay, and while it wasn't easy, you could crank the wheels up or down. When it was necessary, the engineer would do that cranking, unless of course he was injured or wounded. Also, we had fuel in the wings, and if you didn't keep the gas distributed evenly between the wings, your ship might dip down on the right or left side, wherever there was more gas and more weight. You could switch gas from one wing to the other to make sure the ship flew

36

straight, and that was another job for the engineer, to keep the plane balanced.

Besides all that, the engineer was the top turret gunner. The top turret had great visibility and range for firing—three hundred and sixty degrees all around and overhead—but that meant there was a problem: to fire in different directions the whole turret had to move—the gun itself was stationary—and for a while there was a possibility that a guy could accidentally be aiming at his own ship and even shoot it down.

That might sound stupid if not impossible, but when you're focused on a target, you have tunnel vision, and there's all sorts of things you might not notice, not even your own aircraft. So they needed to design a gun that had a cut-out, and they did, quite successfully— when the gun was aimed at its own ship, it would stop firing automatically, even though the trigger was depressed, and when the gun was aimed away from the ship and the trigger was depressed, it would start firing again automatically. It was a very complicated system, but it really worked.

Behind the bomb bay there was a little room for the radio operator, Ron Moellering. It was his job to monitor the intercom system on the plane. Also to use a home base signal, like from London, say, that he could pick up and determine the plane's latitude and longitude to relay to the navigator, then the navigator could set the course. He stayed in touch with headquarters and kept them informed of the state of the mission—which target was bombed (there was an A target and a B target in case we couldn't hit the A target)—and the results. He listened for messages from headquarters concerning any changes in plans. Finally, he also manned a fifty-caliber machine gun that he fired through an aperture in the fuselage. Not a lot of range—couldn't fire down—but everything helped.

Next back and hanging from the belly of the plane was the ball turret, which sort of looked like a big bulb made out of aluminum and plexiglass with two machine guns sticking out of it. The ball turret worked like the top turret—the guns were stationary and the turret swiveled all around, three hundred and sixty degrees—so the gunners ran the same danger of shooting at their own ship until that cut-out was invented.

The gunner didn't get into the ball turret until the plane had taken off. Being underneath like that wasn't the safest place to be on a takeoff, or a landing either, for that matter, and it was so uncomfortable you wanted the gunner to be in that turret for as little time as possible. It was very hard to get into—you had to squeeze in—and once he got in, the gunner's knees would be up by his shoulders—a tight fit, almost fetal—and he would be in there like that all by himself for hours and hours. The ball turret gunner was almost always the smallest guy in the crew, and if he was claustrophobic… well, he couldn't be claustrophobic. He'd die of panic.

Harry Swinger was our ball turret gunner.

I was a waist gunner. Initially, for the first couple years of the war, there were two of us, one on each side of the plane, but by the time I was flying missions, the summer of '44, there was only one, partly because of a shortage of men, and partly because the Luftwaffe, the German air corps, was not the threat it had been. You shot the waist guns out of large windows on the sides of the plane, a little behind the middle of the fuselage, so those guns were flexible, you could move them around, unlike the turret guns, but they didn't have the cut-out feature, which meant you could accidentally shoot the wing off your airplane, for example, or the tail, so that was a danger, but the flexibility was necessary for hitting a moving target. You just had to be careful's all.

The waist gunner stood through the whole mission—which could last as long as twelve hours—and the footing was not solid like it was on the ground or a regular floor because of the curvature of the fuselage and the turbulence you encountered when flying. Turbulence from air currents, from flak, and from the wash of all those propellers in the formation—all that made just standing difficult, and it made shooting a fifty-caliber machine gun, which had a considerable kick-back—it made shooting it with any accuracy even harder.

At the very back of the plane was the tail-gunner, Bob Fox. He manned two fifty-caliber machine guns in very close quarters, though not as close as the ball turret gunner. The tail gunner couldn't sit or stand—he was on his knees for most of the flight. The guns were mounted in a special cradle-like gizmo, and a little stick came up that he pushed around to make them turn any way he wanted them to go. It was funny looking, kind of like a joy stick, but it worked.

The B-17 was called the fortress of the sky. Besides the bombs it was armed with thirteen fifty-caliber machine guns. The entire plane was a really lethal weapon. And it could take an enormous amount of punishment. Obviously it wasn't built for comfort. It was built exclusively for bombing and shooting the enemy.

A weird thing happened the first time I fired the gun in flight on a B-17. We were going past targets that were on the ground and shooting at them. When the first target came up and I aimed and pulled the trigger, the gun shot only one round then stopped, even though I had the trigger fully depressed, whereas, since it was a *machine* gun, it was supposed to keep firing until I released the trigger. So I tried it again—recharged the gun, pulled the trigger, and again it fired one shot and stopped.

Well, this was something they didn't teach me how to deal with in gunnery school, so I called Bob Fox, the tail gunner. "Bob," I said, "come on up here, I've got a problem and I don't know how to figure it out. I want to take a close look at it." He came up to the waist and I said, "I want you to shoot this gun so I can look at the mechanism and see if I can figure out what the problem is."

Well, I got close so I could see, and he shot it, and just like what happened with me, it shot one round and stopped, but I could feel something in my face, like someone had thrown salt in it, or sand. I said, "Shoot it again, Bob."

He said, "Okay," racked it back and shot it again. Same thing. Then I just happened to look over my shoulder and said,

"Hey, Bob! Would you look at that?"

He looked and said, "What the hell!"

What we saw was two holes in the side of the plane. We scrutinized the barrel and figured out what was happening: it had a rupture in it, so, instead of coming out the end of the barrel, the bullet was coming out the side. What I felt in my face was the burning powder from the bullet. That was something the books didn't tell us about.

Now, you have to understand that the barrel was not permanently attached to the gun; you screwed it on and off. You picked it up at the dispensary, like the

bombardier did with the Norden, and took it to the plane

and screwed it on; when you landed you unscrewed the

barrel, looked it over to make sure it was in good shape,

then you took it back to the dispensary, and they were

also supposed to look it over. I have to say, whoever

gave me that barrel must have known it wasn't right,

unless he was blind (which he wasn't!) because there was

this clearly visible hole in the side of it. Why he would

give me a barrel like that I never found out—maybe he

was just careless, incompetent—and I hadn't thought to

look it over first because no one had ever said a thing

about the possibility of a ruptured barrel. After that I

always looked over the barrels they gave me.

But here's the kicker. When I took the barrel

back to the dispensary, they wanted to charge me a

hundred dollars for it. Which is a lot even now, but in

1944, when a private's monthly income was fifty

bucks…! So I said, "What! You gave me something

that was bad and you're going to charge me for it? I

could have got killed with this damn thing!"

They said, "Sorry, but that's a hundred bucks."

I went and told Bob Felgar, the pilot, about it—a

lieutenant pilot had a lot more clout than a sergeant

gunner—and he said, "Let *me* talk to them." So he and I

went over there and he told them, "What the hell's the

matter with you guys? You almost killed this man,

giving him an inferior piece of equipment, and now you

want to *charge* him for it? He oughta charge *you*! He's

not going to pay you a hundred dollars—he's not going to

pay you *one*!—so just forget about it." And they did.

I'm not sure why, but I never told anybody that

that happened. Maybe I'd have felt like a snitch. I was

eighteen, remember. But I'd bet it happened other times
to other guys. Maybe even in combat, though I hope not.

In March we went from Ardmore to Kearney,
Nebraska. It was a transfer point where we were supposed to pick up a B-17 and fly to our base in England.
Well, there were plenty of B-17's there, ready to fly, but
the weather was too bad to fly in. Heavy snow still on
the ground, rain and sleet and such, even though it was
spring on the calendar. We sat around for two weeks,
until the brass said we couldn't wait any longer and
ordered us to Camp Kilmer in Camden, New Jersey.
Back to New Jersey!

They gave us a physical before shipping out.
Gave us shots for all kinds of things. I had a couple of
cavities in my molars, but instead of filling them, they
pulled the teeth out. Said they didn't have time to fill

them. Three teeth they pulled. That made me really

mad.

We went by train to Camp Kilmer, and from there

we went to England, not in a B-17 as we expected, but by

boat! We thought that was pretty funny, air force guys

being transported by train and boat. While we were

waiting to take off, the brass decided to eliminate one of

the waist gunners, cutting the crew from ten men to nine.

The reason was they were running out of gunners and

couldn't keep up with the demand for more. Also, by

this time in the war, as I said, the Luftwaffe was not the

danger it had been, so they figured one waist gunner

could handle both sides of the plane, and it turned out

they were right.

So it was between me and the other waist gun-

ner—I don't' recall his name—but he was considerably

older than the rest of us, married with a couple of kids, so we decided, all nine of us, that he should be the one to be cut. I was actually glad that I could stay on.

I suppose I should call the boat we went across on a ship, but it didn't deserve the dignity. It was a real... how should I say it? Before the war it was used to haul meat from Australia to England and back. A meat cargo ship, just carrying more meat, you could say. It was Australian, and the captain and crew were Aussies, and civilians at that, not soldiers.

The food was terrible. The first day out they served us this incredibly nasty concoction of tomatoes and liver. Stewed liver. Now, there are people who get airsick, of course, just like some people get seasick or carsick, but none of us guys on that boat—who'd been in flight training for weeks and weeks, don't forget—no one had gotten airsick, but now a lot of us, including yours truly, we took one look at that concoction, and got one whiff, and headed straight for the rails, throwing up like crazy. What we got wasn't seasick—it was stewed-liver-sick.

There were a couple of vending machines on the boat, one with Pepsi's, one with M & M's, and that's about what we lived on, the ship food was so bad. For diversion we would put our empty bottles under our hammocks—that's another thing: we slept in hammocks instead of bunk beds—and while we were sleeping, and the ship rolled back and forth, the bottles would roll as well, rattling all the way across and back, across and back. It was funny and kind of fun—it seemed like the bottles had a life of their own—but it was also bother-some and made it hard to sleep, which was hard enough anyway, sleeping in a hammock.

It took us two weeks to get to England. It took so long because we were going across the Atlantic in May,

1944, and it was full of German U-boat, submarines, which was their main weapon in that part of the world, offensive and defensive, and they were shooting down ships left and right. And we were in a large fleet, many ships in a bunch, which made us easier to detect. The Atlantic was just full of these submarines. Our ships had equipment that could pick up the sounds of the German subs, just as their subs could pick up the sounds of our ships, and when our crew detected a sub nearby, they shut down the engines and we came to a standstill. For hours, sometimes a whole day at a time, nobody could make any noise whatsoever. Couldn't hit or even touch a wall, couldn't run water or flush, because the Nazis could pick up the slightest sounds with their instruments, get a line on you, and blow you right out of the water. That was kind of exciting, not knowing what was going to happen. I kind of enjoyed the suspense. Today I'd probably be stressed out.

The Germans docked and built and repaired their submarines in these massive concrete structures that our bombs couldn't penetrate, couldn't destroy, they were so thick, otherwise we would have bombed them out. What we wound up doing—not me, but our fighter pilots—was take out the subs themselves with rockets.

Anyway, needless to say, I'm glad to say, we made it across in one piece.

PART 2 – COMBAT

We finally landed in England and were sent to Kimbolton Airfield near Bedford, which was about fifty miles north of London. On the base we stayed in Quonset huts, those buildings with a domed roof made of corrugated metal that they could throw together in like no time. Thirty inch beds, a few shelves for our clothes and stuff. A separate building where we could take a shower and take care of our other personal needs, you might say. The mess hall was also in a separate building. Kimbolton wasn't the Ritz.

The Germans were bombing London with V1 and V2 rockets by then. These rockets had no pilots; they were unmanned. They had an X amount of fuel in them—the Germans knew how much fuel it would take to fly to London, so the rockets ran out of fuel when they got there and fell on the city. When you were on the ground and you heard one approaching, then the motor stopped, you knew it was coming down. Those rockets did a lot of damage—blew up a lot of buildings and roads, killed a lot of people. Some nights we could hear them in Bedford, and see the flashes of the explosions, fifty miles away!

One night we were on leave in London—it was the only leave I remember having while in England—and we got a cab and told the driver to take us to a pub where we could get a cold beer, as opposed to the customary room-temperature ale there—and he told us how used to the V1's and V2's he was, unlike us Yanks, nothing to get in a panic about.   Then we heard one approach, heard the motor stop, and without a word the cabbie slammed on the brakes, jumped out of the car and took off running, leaving us in the cab in the middle of the street. The rocket exploded only a couple of blocks away. So the rockets were nothing to panic about, just run like hell from.

That night we stayed in a hotel. As we were going up to our rooms, we were passing people going down carrying blankets and pillows. We wondered what they were up to, if there was a big slumber party going on somewhere. In the room the window was open, and it was cold, so I closed it. Later some rockets started falling, and one of them hit close enough to shatter the window I had closed. Then we figured out what all those people were doing: they were going to the basement, not for a slumber party, but as a bomb shelter. I caught hell from the front desk for closing the window—the reason they left it open was so it wouldn't get shattered—but as far as I was concerned, they should have explained that in the first place. Like the cabbie could have told us to run for it.

In Bedford we had no interaction with the townies to speak of. There was one pub, but it was so crowded you could hardly get inside. Customers would pass the pints hand-to-hand to the people buying them, and pass the money from the customers back to the bar, because there was no way to get to the bar and get a drink directly from the bartender. But we hardly ever went there. Mostly we stuck around the base because if we weren't flying, we were recovering from flying. And when we weren't recovering from flying we were keeping track of the planes coming back from missions.

We called that "sweating it out"—sweating it out for your buddies, hoping they'd make it back. And to see some of those ships coming back with parts of their wings gone, engines missing, tails shot up and in tatters, fuselages riddled with holes like Swiss cheese, just about anything you can imagine, and yet still flying in. Belly landings. Amazing stuff, and terrible. The guys who didn't make it back, you'd watch soldiers get their stuff to mail back home, guys you'd bunked with, talked with, now gone. And you knew their families would be receiving a telegram or a letter saying their boy was missing in action—that was sad. Hard.

We had been assigned to the 379th Bomb Group of the 8th Air Force. I was really happy about that because the 379th was topnotch, a topnotch group—they had the best record for the number of missions they flew and bombs they dropped and the accuracy of their strikes.

Almost immediately upon arriving our pilot Felgar was selected to make a test run. What it was I don't know—he was sworn to secrecy, apparently—and he never told us where they went or what they did. That's one thing about the military you have to learn to deal with—there's always a whole lot you don't know. Bob was about five years older than I was—which means he was only twenty-three—but he had a lot of experience flying before the war. He was probably one of the best B-17 pilots they ever had. Maybe I just felt loyal to him because I flew with him on so many missions and he always did such a great job. I felt that if anything happened he could and would take care of the situation.

While waiting to fly our first mission—that's *another* thing about being in the military: you spend a lot of time waiting—we practiced formation flying. Colonel Maurice Preston was Commander of the 379th, and he was a stickler for flying tight formations, the tighter the better because the tighter the safer.

Our first mission happened to be D–Day. June 6, 1944. We took off around nine in the morning and flew over the beach to bomb German gun emplacements. I never saw so many ships and boats in my whole life. Thousands, it seemed, as far as the eye could see, even from on high. We could see the boats in the harbor and the men landing on the beach and the fighting that was going on. You couldn't make out any particular soldier you were looking at—we were too high for that, probably around fourteen thousand feet, which was actually low for a B-17, but still…. I felt like a spectator of an epic event. There were no German airplanes in the sky to look out for, surprisingly. As we found out later, the Germans had prepared for a much bigger invasion up around Calais; they had been tricked into thinking

Normandy was like a diversion. So the resistance they had at Normandy was all on the ground. It was an experience that I knew I would never ever have again, seeing all those boats, all those soldiers—it was something else.

Another thing I saw was really disturbing—once past the beach, American gliders littered the ground, meadows and woods. They were broken, upside down, lying sidewise and every which way. Hundreds of them. Turned out, they had been filled with soldiers and equipment and had been hauled in by C-54 transport planes to drop behind the German lines, but they were so vulnerable the Germans could shoot them down with ease. It was like they were on a suicide mission. Like I said, really disturbing, all those soldiers wounded and dead. Mostly dead.

After the first mission, we flew back to

Kimbolton, rested up, then took off again. That time we

flew further inland and dropped five hundred pound

bombs on bridges, to keep the Germans from moving

reinforcements to the front. Not easily, anyway. We got

back from that mission around dusk, which in England,

in June, is *late*. Pushing eleven. A full day's work.

Here's how a mission worked. It began when

they got you out of bed. It might be four o'clock in the

morning, five o'clock. Sometimes you knew when you

were going to go on one, sometimes not. You'd get

dressed and go to the mess hall for breakfast. They

served just about anything you wanted—bacon and eggs,

omelets, biscuits, pancakes, waffles, French toast—and it

was smart to eat as much as you could, because once you

were airborne you couldn't eat, except for a chocolate bar

from your mess kit. Worse yet, you weren't going to eat

again for the rest of the day, because when you got back, which could be ten or twelve hours later, the mess hall was closed. Even though the mess hall crew *knew* plane crews were coming back hungry as hell. It made no sense! You couldn't even get a cheese sandwich.

After breakfast you'd go to the briefing room where they would lay out the mission for you. They had a couple of big maps, which they hung with thumb tacks and ribbons, to show you where you were going, what your target was, and what the weather might be like. If the target was covered—that is, covered over with clouds so you couldn't see it—you were to get as close to it as you could guess, go on radar and just drop the bombs. If you were going to Munich, for example, and the target was covered, you would drop the bombs on the city in general rather than on the assigned target in or around the city. We made three or four trips to Munich, and every time it was covered except the last, when we could aim at the intended target.

Usually a fighter had already gone over the area in advance—an air scout—and gotten a read on the weather and taken photos, to give us as good an idea as possible of what the area looked like.

The room was always tense and very smoky—almost everyone smoked back then—but the briefing itself was very organized, precise. After this general briefing, there were often some specific briefings for certain positions—pilots with pilots, navigators with navigators, and so on.

After the briefings the bombardier picked up the bombsight from the dispensary. Like I said, this bombsight, the Norden, was state of the art, gyro stabilized, linked electronically to the auto-pilot, extremely accurate. It was regarded as top-secret, so valuable that the bombardier was escorted to the plane by an armed guard. In case you got shot down, it was to be destroyed so the Germans couldn't get it. Likewise, when a mission was over the bombardier took it back to the dispensary and checked it in.

While in training I had to check out the barrel for my fifty-caliber from the dispensary the same, if you recall, but once in England and flying missions the barrels were fixed, which was fine by me—one less thing to have to deal with.

After we got out of the mess hall and were heading for the airplane, our tail gunner, Bob Fox, was always looking for a little box. One time I said, "What the hell are you doing, Bob? You're always looking for a box after we eat—what do you do with that?"

And he said, "Well, usually before we get to high altitude I do my morning business in the box. And when we get to fifteen, twenty thousand feet, my business freezes up like a brick, so when the bombardier shouts 'Bombs away' I say 'Bombs away number two!' and throw it out the camera hatch back there. I always imagine some German looking up and getting gob-smacked in the face with it."

We were driven to the plane in a Jeep. We got into our flight gear: fleece-lined, electrically heated, armored flight suits; heated felt booties that fit into our regular boots; heated gloves; fleece-lined helmets, oxygen masks. We put on parachutes, or else we carried our parachutes along. And each of us got an escape kit that contained small amounts of several currencies—French francs, Belgian francs, Dutch guilders; a silk map of the target area in case we got shot down, to escape capture if possible; a fake ID; some Benzedrine, which was a stimulant in case we needed some stimulation; some concentrated food tablets; a compass; and a chocolate bar.

This may sound crazy, but eating that chocolate bar while airborne wasn't easy. When you got high up, over ten, fifteen thousand feet, you had to put on your oxygen mask, which covered your nose and came down over your chin. The higher you got, the colder it got, and after a while ice would form around your mouth and your chin and down your neck—you know, from the moisture in your breath—ice so thick you had to continually scrape it off with a finger—it just froze right to your mask—and that made eating that chocolate bar really tough.

Some guys would grease their faces so their oxygen masks wouldn't freeze to their skin.

Incidentally, if you had to pee, you'd go into the bomb bay on this little cat-walk, about four, five inches wide, that went from one end of the bomb bay to the other—it was sort of like a balance beam—and there were no railings, you'd just grab anything you could get hold of. There was a rubber hose with a funnel on it, and that's where you went, *after* you had peeled your flight suit off. It was difficult. And you didn't want to freeze your pecker off, so you went only when you really had to.

After we'd get into the plane and into our positions, the bombardier would climb out on the catwalk over the bomb bay with a container of fuses that he screwed into the noses and tails of the bombs with a wrench. With the fuses in, the bombs were alive. This was a delicate operation that could literally blow up in your face, and blow up everything else in the vicinity. It happened once in a while (though never at Kimbolton while we were there), blasting the plane and crew, and nearby planes and crews as well. Could kill as many as forty, fifty men.

Once the bombs were loaded we waited to take off, a wait that could take several hours with so many planes going up. The planes took off right on the heels of one another, about thirty seconds apart. Because it was England, we often took off in heavy fog and rain—lousy visibility. Taking off in those conditions was very hairy. Then, when we were finally up, above the cloud cover where we could see, we made our formations and headed for our destination.

The ball turret gunner got in his little turret after we crossed the English Channel, and he'd be scrunched up in there until we got back to the Channel, five, six hours later, eight or nine. When he could finally get out, it was murder, he was so stiff. The tail gunner, too—

after spending hours on his knees like that, he was almost as stiff as the ball-turret gunner.

As for me, a waist gunner, there was no place for me to sit, and I was standing on a rounded surface. Really difficult. So I found a piece of armor plate, about an eighth of an inch thick and about two feet long, and put it on the floor, to have something flat to stand on. Then after the mission I would catch hell—they'd say I wasn't supposed to do that. I said I had to have some-thing steady and flat to stand on, plus that plate could help protect me from any flak that hit the bottom of the ship. And they said that if the plane got hit and that plate was flopping around like a loose cannon, it was an added danger. And I said it wouldn't flop around if I was standing on it.

It became like a game. They would take it out, I would put it back in. Their protests were pretty much pro forma, actually. They always put it where they knew I could find it, somewhere in the hangar. As it happened, no harm came of having it in the plane.

After we dropped our bombs we turned to go back to the base. You stayed in formation because there was still flak to deal with, and the possibility of German fighter planes. Unless you couldn't, of course—if you had an engine out, or two engines. You could still fly, but you couldn't keep up with the rest of the formation. This happened quite a bit. Mostly from losing engines from the flak. A lot of planes, of course, went down.

When we got back we went to interrogation, which is what they called the debriefing. We lined up going into a room, and when it came our turn we told them whatever we could about the mission we'd just completed—how much resistance, how much damage we'd suffered, how many planes did we see go down, how many parachutes did we see, how the bombing went—that sort of thing. How, if we saw smoke rising a thousand feet, we knew we had hit a target that had fuel. Or how we had hit railroad junctions, bridges, things like that. Then they'd give us a glass of whiskey. Old Grand-dad or whatever. Just one shot. If you had a friend who didn't drink, you could get two shots.

I can't say often enough how unbelievably durable the B-17 was. Sometimes, for example, a plane's hydraulic system got shot up or shattered from flak, and they'd come in to land and discover that they couldn't lower the wheels. Sometimes the engineer could get the wheels down with the crank, sometimes not, depending on the extent of the damage. If not, then the plane would have to make a belly landing. Sometimes a ship was riddled by bullets and flak with vital parts missing—like the tail assembly, or the entire nose, or much of a wing, and the fuselage broken. *Broken*, the front and back barely intact! And often engines out of commission, as many as three, and oxygen systems and controls shot up, and fires in different areas of the plane, and so many bullet holes the plane looked like a sieve, and still they made it back to the base.

We never had to make a belly landing ourselves, but we did make a hairy landing once when we ran into trouble and out of fuel. We were returning from Munich and one of our engines got hit, so Felgar feathered it— meaning he turned the engine off so the propellers wouldn't rotate, and then he set the propellers sideways, to reduce wind resistance. Then another engine over- heated, so he feathered it and we were running on just two. When we were nearing the English Channel we were so low on fuel that Felgar told us to start throwing everything out. We threw all the guns out, and the

ammo, armor plate, flak jackets, the plate I stood on—
anything that weighed anything. Then he said we were
going to try to make it over the Channel.

By that time a third engine gave out, so he
feathered *it,* and now we were running on *one* engine.
We were almost in a glide, you might say. He said he
thought we could make it, but if it turned out we couldn't
he was going to ask for volunteers to bail out, to cut the
weight down. Bail out into the Channel. But we did
make it, over the Channel and just short of the runway
where he landed the doggone thing.

Only now it was on fire, stuff burning, all the
wires popping and spitting sparks and flames. We got
out, everybody got out, and started running because we
thought the plane was going to blow up. While we were
running a lieutenant came by in a Jeep and hollered,

"Hey you guys, come on back and help us put this fire out!"

Felgar hollered right back at him: "Go to hell—we're not going anywhere near that thing!" As it happened, it didn't blow up—not enough fuel for that to happen—but it never flew again, that's for sure.

One of our early missions was scary as hell. Some fighter planes from the Luftwaffe were waiting for us, but instead of attacking us directly, what they did was fly alongside us but far enough away from our formation to be out of our guns' range. They were going the same speed and the same direction we were going, and they were radioing this information back down to the flak gunners, how high we were, how fast we were going, so the gunners could zero their guns in on us. Those gunners were good. They took down a lot of B-17's and B-24's. Fortunately, they didn't hit us that day, even with the assistance of the Luftwaffe, but they came close. Like I said, scary as hell.

Flak was our main danger. Flak was shells that were fired from the ground by eighty-eight caliber cannons. The shells would explode in puffs of flame and black smoke, blasting shrapnel all over the place. Sometimes there was so much flak it looked like you could walk on it. And if it exploded close enough, the concussion would shake the ship, making it bump and jostle up and down, side to side, and I had to keep my balance through all that while standing, sometimes grabbing on to anything I could get my hands on. You could hear the shrapnel hit the bottom of the ship, like someone throwing gravel against a tin roof. I would move around a little to try to avoid it—say it was hitting here, I would move a couple of steps over to there. Of course I never really *knew* where it might hit next, but still, I could at least *try* to escape it. But if you were a ball turret gunner, you better just be lucky: you couldn't move a bit.

The first time I went up and saw flak like that, I said to myself, "Holy mackerel, how can we fly through all this stuff?" And in my mind I was saying, "Yea, though I walk through the valley of the shadow of death, I will fear no evil. Thy rod and thy staff will comfort me." I mean, it *was* the valley of death. For real.

Another thing that made flak so dangerous: when the bombardier in the lead plane got the target in his bombsight, the plane would shoot off a flare to notify all the other planes, then the Norden kicked in the autopilot so that we all flew on a steady course, a straight line, for at least fifty seconds, which made us for that time—and fifty seconds can be a very very long time—that made us like sitting ducks for the German gunners. And for German fighter pilots too, if there were any. But to bomb with any sort of accuracy that was what we had to do. When the lead plane's bombardier released his bombs, all the other planes released theirs. We called that "blanket" or "carpet" bombing, since so many planes were releasing their bombs at once. When the bombs were released you could feel the plane surge and lift, naturally, since we were suddenly four to eight tons lighter.

We always dropped all the bombs, even if we weren't on target, because you didn't want to fly back carrying live bombs—the weight slowed you down, and if you got hit, they would make matters worse. As in *way* worse! And you sure as hell didn't want to land with them on board!

We knew that the mortality rate for flyers over Europe was really high. Like two-thirds, or something like that. That the more missions you flew, the greater the chances of getting hit. That the first ten or eleven missions the chances of survival were about fifty percent, and after eleven or so that rate went down, progressively. And you saw planes go down, you'd count how many men got out of them and how many didn't. And at the base, those planes coming in with dead and wounded aboard would fire off a red flare, and they were allowed to land first, so the wounded could get tended to as soon as possible—you'd see them getting carried off the planes and taken away. And you'd see which planes didn't make it back at all, see the empty bunks. We watched, we prayed, we counted, so yeah, we were aware how many planes and men didn't make it back, and how many who did were wounded if not dead.

It was tough to take, but we were really young, remember—eighteen, nineteen, twenty, not quite convinced of our personal mortality. And with so much death around you, you sort of pushed it to the back of your mind. You didn't let yourself think about it before a mission—you just couldn't—so yeah, you were scared, needless to say, but you weren't in a funk with fear, weren't paralyzed. During a mission, when you were being attacked, you could get the heebie-jeebies, but you could manage them by focusing on your duties, on getting there, dropping the bombs, and getting back. Usually the heavy fear would come, if it came, afterwards. Then, going back over the mission in your mind, you could get the shakes, have trouble sleeping, panic attacks.

Getting hit was a whole different story, of course. So much fear and panic going on you could smell it, taste it, swallow it. On a percentage basis, direct hits were rare, I'd say—the number of hits per the number of shells shot—but the Germans had thousands of those eighty-eights, so there were still a lot of direct hits. Way too many as far as we were concerned, of course.

I think I've said that by the time we got over there, the Luftwaffe was no threat, so many of them had been shot down. They had enough airplanes, but they had only a few pilots left, and they were even younger than we were, and had hardly had any training. For our fighter pilots, shooting the German fighters was almost like target practice. I remember one mission we went on—it was to Munich—it seemed they used everything they had, every plane and every pilot, because this was the third time we went to Munich, I think, and the Germans were getting really ticked off about it. But their fighters couldn't get up to our elevation, which could be as high as thirty, thirty-five thousand feet. I don't think they even got a shot at our B-17's. And we had an armada of fighter planes—P-38's, P-51's, P-47's—all going after the German planes, often two on one, taking the Germans out left and right. After that I don't think we ever saw another German fighter.

In fact, in all my thirty-three missions I never had to fire at one German plane.

Almost the last mission we flew, the Germans had perfected a jet fighter plane—I forget the name of it now—that flew five, six hundred miles an hour, whereas our fastest plane, the P-51 Mustang, flew in combat around three hundred, three hundred fifty miles an hour. We heard this sound—*sssssshhhheeeeeuuuu!*—and barely caught a glimpse of it, it went by so fast. So fast you couldn't hope to train a gun on it. *So* fast! We only saw a couple of them, thank God—they were something brand new—so our biggest problem was still flak. To counter flak we had what was called "chaff." It was a metallic, shiny-like paper, something like tin foil or tinsel, like the icicles you hang on Christmas trees, all

wrapped up in bundles. We'd throw these bundles out—

that was one of my jobs, to throw those bundles out of

the window—and they would break and all this tinsel

would float down to earth. The eighty-eights that the

Germans used for the high altitudes we flew at had a

radar beam that would track the planes they were aimed

at, so they could set their guns for that distance and

height precisely, but the chaff would reflect the beams

the same as the planes, and the gunners couldn't tell if the

radar blips they were looking at signified planes or chaff.

And they no longer had enough planes to help them

direct their fire, the way they did on that early mission I

was on.

There was an American woman who was in

Germany before the war and must have liked it there a

lot, because after the war broke out she stayed and

worked for the Nazis, as a radio personality, you could say. Her name was Gertrude, and she had a radio show called "Home Sweet Home" which was broadcast on our wave band, so we listened to her right on the plane, through our headsets, the same ones we used to communicate with each other. We would tune her in while on a mission, because she played music by Glenn Miller, Benny Goodman, Tommy and Jimmy Dorsey, the Andrews Sisters, the Mills Brothers, Duke Ellington, Harry James, and the American pop songs of the day like "A Nightingale Sang in Berkeley Square," and "I'll Be Seeing You," and "Sing Sing Sing."

Sometimes she would comment on what she had just played. Like "Till Then," where the singer's pleading for his girl friend to wait for him "till then," then meaning back home, and she would say, "We know you, fellas, and I'm sure you're yearning plenty for someone.

But I just wonder if she *is* waiting till then, if she isn't seeing some 4-F back home. Why don't you just give up and go home, go back to your loved ones?" (4-F, by the way, was the classification for anyone who couldn't pass the physical for the armed service.) She said lots of stuff like that, in a real sexy sultry voice. Like Tokyo Rose in the Pacific.

"Dirty Gertie, the Bitch from Berlin," we called her. Others called her Axis Sally. "You know, boys, your real enemy is the Russians. Since you can't defeat us, why don't you join us so we can defeat the Russians together?" We could shut her off—we didn't have to listen—but we liked her voice and the music she played. As for her message, though, we thought it was stupid.

But it could get a little weird, listening to her. We brought our plane back to England one time with the left wing shattered and two engines knocked out, and there was a lot of other damage as well. By the way, it was amazing how the mechanics could fix those things. The planes could be *mutilated,* beyond repair, you'd think, and time after time those mechanics got them fixed up and flying again. They were the backbone of the air corps, really—worked all hours day and night. I don't think they got the credit they deserved.

Pretty soon we got our plane back with the motors running and a new wing. Like most other planes until the end, our plane was camouflage colored on top, to blend into the terrain when looking down at them, as a German fighter would, and a kind of light blue on the bottom, to blend into the sky when looking up at them, as the German gunners did. But our new wing was bright shiny silver. It really stood out. Well, the next time we flew to Munich Dirty Gertie said, "Ah, I see you, Silver Wing!" I mean, she had us in view while she was broadcasting! I'll tell you, that felt strange. But we liked

the name she gave us, so we adopted it for our ship and

dropped the name we had been using, Fearless Fosdick,

which was the name I had suggested.

Fearless Fosdick was a cartoon character by Al

Capp, the guy who did the comic strip Li'l Abner. Fos-

dick was a takeoff on Dick Tracy, the cartoon cop with a

two-way wrist radio who tracked down and nabbed bad

guys, and we liked Fearless Fosdick as a name because it

made the Germans seem a little like cartoons, like

clowns. But Silver Wing sounded kind of like a badge

of respect from the enemy, an honor of sorts, so we

adopted it.

When we flew to Munich again, Dirty Gertie

said, "Ah, Silver Wing, we're waiting for you —you're

really going to get it this time." That was the time all

those German planes came up, and our guys knocked

them out of the sky like crazy. They were having fun. That was the last big air battle, and I'm surprised there wasn't more conversation about it, how many planes were shot down, the total damage. The next time we flew to Munich, though, when the Luftwaffe offered no resistance, Dirty Gertie was on the same message even though it no longer made sense: "Ah, Silver Wing, you're back again. We're ready for you this time. Give up. You're not going to make it. You'll wish you'd stayed home." We wondered why *she* didn't give up.

Some of these B-17's, like the Memphis Belle, actually became famous, along with their crews, because I don't know how, but they put in twenty-five missions and everybody came out alive. No wounds even. And flew the same airplane for every mission! That's almost impossible. The vast majority of us never flew twenty-five missions in one airplane. What usually happened was you flew altogether in four or five. And often the planes were an assembly of parts from several planes cobbled together so they could go back out.

Our squad got all our planes back to England, except the one we went down in, but it was *planes* we got back, more than one. Which was one reason we didn't get the name of our ship printed on the nose with a cartoon drawing of Fearless Fosdick, like so many did. We never figured we'd fly just one plane on all our missions, so decorating one didn't seem worth the trouble.

In addition to waist gunner I was also what they called the armament gunner. Now, the bombs on the plane were hung on racks, racks that could handle all that weight, anywhere from eight to seventeen thousand pounds. When the bombardier got the target in sight, he'd hit a button to open the bomb bay doors, then hit another to release the bombs, but sometimes the bombs would get hung up—you know, maybe they didn't get hung quite right, or the super cold temperature froze them up—and when that happened, my job was to crawl out on the catwalk, then go down into the bay, which was open—you could see right through it, *fall* right through it—and when we hit air pockets and turbulence from flak you could feel the plane moving up and down and side-wise, and the wind blowing, and the cold, and there wasn't anything to hang on to—all that got a guy's atten-tion, let me tell you!—but those bombs, which were hanging by hooks, had to be released, so I had to pry the hooks loose with a screwdriver, by hand. I had to do that job a couple of times, and twice was enough.

The flights were often long and tedious, until we got near the target anyway, so a little diversion went a long way to pass the time. I had a good memory for jokes and anecdotes, so I'd tell stories and jokes over our

intercom system.

What do Nazis eat for breakfast?
Luftwaffles.

What did the Mayor of Paris say to the German army
when they entered Paris?
Table for a hundred thousand, m'sieur?

Hey, anyone interested in a used Italian rifle for sale?
Never been shot, dropped only once.

Irwin, the co-pilot, said I was the comic relief on the

ship, and to keep it up. Which I did. I've always loved

to sing, so I would sing, too, songs like "Don't Fence Me

In" and "I've Got a Lovely Bunch of Coconuts" and "Ac

Cent Tchu Ate the Positive" and "Boogie Woogie Bugle

Boy" and "Don't Sit Under the Apple Tree." And

sometimes Dirty Gertie would break in to say something

like, "She's not waiting, boys. She's sitting under an

apple tree with some 4- F," or, "She's getting her

coconuts from someone else, boys, some guy back home.

Go on back, while you still can." Etcetera.

I would carry on like that till we got near our

target or started running into flak, and Felgar would

break in and say, "Okay, Carl, we'll take over now."

Our shortest missions were into France, a few

hours. Our longest, when we flew into Germany, could

last as long as twelve hours. Berlin was the farthest.

A formation was made of many groups, and each

group had a marking on their airplane, like Triangle 25.

So while you were flying and saw a group of airplanes,

you could look at their tail and see what group they were.

Well, one group had a real bad reputation. It was the

100th. The scuttlebutt for their reputation was, they got

in trouble on one of their missions and had to fall out of

formation. They were losing altitude. Then they saw

two German fighters flying alongside them. When they

saw those fighters, the pilot put the wheels down. Now,

when you put the wheels down like that, that's a sign of

surrender, a white flag. So the fighters moved closer to

escort the ship down to where it could land and the crew

could be taken as prisoners. Well, the pilot told the crew,

"What the hell—we don't want to be taken

prisoner" or something to that effect, and they said,

"Well, what do you want us to do?" and he said,

"Hell, shoot 'em down!"

So they shot both those escort planes down. I

mean, they were so close you couldn't miss them—didn't

even have to lead—all you had to do was point the gun at

them and pull the trigger. After that, any time there were

any German fighters around, they would single out and

follow the Bloody 100th, as the group came to be called,

and give them the works. They were a special target, and they suffered a lot of damage and casualties.

Well, I forget what mission it was, our eighteenth or something like that, and it was to Berlin. This was only the second time Berlin had been bombed, I believe. And I've gotta say, hitting Berlin was *especially* gratifying, because we'd heard that Goering, the fatso nutso head of the Luftwaffe, had said that if we ever flew into Germany his name wasn't Goering—he could be called Meyer—and here we were, not only bombing targets in Germany, but bombing the capitol and very heart of the country, Berlin! And hit 'em we did. It was an all-out mission. Anything that had wings on it was in the air and was going to Berlin, over a thousand bombers and nine hundred fighters. The convoy was three hundred miles long. When the lead planes started dropping bombs on the city, the planes at the tail end were still in Holland. The bombing lasted over three hours.

Unfortunately, our plane got started on the wrong foot that day. We were going down the runway and were about to take off when the landing gear on the left side of the plane collapsed and we went *sssshhhhhhoooooofffffff* veering off the runway and plowing into the dirt and weeds alongside it. Felgar called the tower and told them what happened. The tower said, "Do not leave the airplane. We will have you in the air in fifteen or twenty minutes." The mechanics came out in like no time with a whole new landing gear, jacked the plane up, took off the damaged landing gear and put a new one on. In fifteen or twenty minutes, just like the tower said. Amazing, those guys were! So we were ready to fly, but had to go back to the head of the runway and start all over again.

So now we're in the air, but we're not with our group—they were long gone, over the Channel or somewhere. Felgar called the tower and said,

"Okay, what do we do now—go on over to the target by ourselves?"

And they said, "No. Just tack on to the next group that goes by. You can be their Tail End Charlie."

Well, who comes by but the Bloody 100th, and Felgar says, "Oh my God, we don't want to be with those suckers," but it was the only thing we could do. So we flew Tail End Charlie with the Bloody 100th—the worst position in the worst squad—but we did manage to drop our bombs without incident. Afterwards, though, instead of staying with them, Felgar didn't want to push our luck, so he decided we should go back by ourselves.

He took the plane up to about thirty thousand feet—out of the 100th's sight, out of their minds—then we started back. After a while he dropped her down from that real high altitude and said to the navigator, "Get us home, Homer—what course should we take?" and Homer gave him the data he needed.

So we're flying along and I'm looking out the side of the airplane, naturally—I was looking all the time—and I say to myself, "Holy criminey, would you look at that!" And then, over the intercom, "Are we anywhere near Paris? That sure as hell looks like the Eiffel Tower to me!"

Felgar said, "Oh my God!" then he said to the navigator, "What the hell kind of course did you set us on, Homer?"

Homer said, "The shortest and fastest, Bob."

Felgar said, "Well, the shortest isn't always the fastest," and sure enough, the Germans started shooting at us. Not really to hit us, I don't think, but to remind us that Paris was an open city; we weren't supposed to be flying over it. So we beat it out of there.

By the time of our thirty-third mission, we had hit various targets in France—in places like Calais, Conde sur Nurreau, Vannes, Fleurs, Orleans, Leon, Lille; we had hit Liege in Belgium, and had hit Hamburg. Bremen, Leipzig, Munich, Zinnositz, Merseberg, Hanover, Berlin, all in Germany. We had bombed bridges, air fields, railroad marshaling yards, aircraft and ball bearing factories, refineries, V-1 missile launch sites, a missile lab, and a jet factory, and, as I've said, we had bombed entire cities like Hamburg, Munich and Berlin.

Hitting the missile launch sites was really tricky. They were extremely well-camouflaged, so what we did, we'd look for skid marks on the ground, where one of the rockets hadn't taken off but had hit the ground and shot off horizontally, leaving a long skid mark. When we saw that, we knew we had our target.

The kind of bomb we used depended on the target we were after. Some of the factories they had in Germany were also well-camouflaged and a lot of them were underground. If they were underground we used a heavier bomb than if we were bombing railroads or bridges. "Anti-personnel bombs" were about a hundred pounds; the next size up was five hundred pounds. They went from there on up. So our particular target for the day dictated the kind of bombs they loaded the plane with.

Bombing by day, we could bomb more precisely than the Brits did at night, but we did not engage in the kind of precision bombing where you went after a single, particular target. None of the B-17's did, to my know-ledge. Like I said, what we did was what we called car-pet bombing. That's why we flew in the formations we did, instead of a long string of airplanes going by drop-ping the bombs one at a time. The lead plane lined the target up, and when it dropped its bombs everybody dropped theirs. Carpet bombing really worked because it was quite a trip to get to the target, and then you wanted to do as much damage as you possibly could. Some of the factories were spread out, and with carpet bombing we could take out the whole complex, plus inflict a lot of what's now called collateral damage, though we didn't regard it as collateral at all. As far as we were con-cerned, the Germans were the enemy, period.

We used incendiary bombs on cities to help our ground troops take them. Incendiaries ignited and spread fires, fires so intense they could reach a thousand degrees and create winds up to a hundred miles an hour, burning

out buildings and houses and water systems, so it was

impossible to put the fires out. When the fires burned

themselves out, our troops could easily move in. For

factories and railroad yards we used heavy bombs, to tear

up the tracks and the engines and whatever else might be

there. For bridges and the like we would use one hun-

dred pounders.

There was another type of bombing, I guess you

could call it, that the fighter planes, the P-38's and P-51's,

engaged in. They had machine guns in the wings and

rockets hanging from the wings, and they were flying all

over the place knocking out trucks and truck convoys and

trains. What they would do, they would first hit the

target with their machine guns, getting a precise line on

it, then make another pass at them and release their

rockets, which would blow the target sky high. Another

thing they did: they would pass over the target and drop gasoline on it, then loop around and strafe it with their machine guns, which would ignite the gas and blow the target up.

So the Germans were getting pounded day and night, left and right.

When we started flying missions on D-Day our limit was set at twenty-five, and then we would be done, like the Memphis Belle crew. But when we got to twenty-four they bumped the number to thirty, and when we got to twenty-seven or twenty-eight they bumped it to thirty-five. And the more you flew, the greater your chances of getting hit. And that's what happened: on our thirty-third mission, we got shot up and had to bail out. That was August 13, a little over two months from when we started.

The co-pilot, Ralph Irwin, had flown a couple of extra missions, so he was up to thirty-five and didn't have to fly anymore. So they assigned us another co-pilot, Henry Benitez, a West Point graduate who had just finished his training. This would be his first mission. From what I understood, his father and his grandfather were West Point people, too, and maybe beyond that. They gave us what was supposed to be an easy mission to fly, where there was little danger of heavy resistance. A "milk run," as we called easy missions. That way Benitez could get some experience before getting into heavier missions, but it turned out that that mission, his first, was also his last. And ours as well.

The mission was to destroy bridges over the Seine in order to help bottle the Germans up for General Patton, who was moving east, toward Germany, with his tanks and troops. And we were to hit the column of retreating German soldiers. One of the reasons we got hit was, we were following a road that the Germans were retreating on, but instead of flying back and forth across the road, as we would have preferred, we had been instructed to fly right up the road, along *with* the column, and to do this much lower than usual, so we could do more damage, but it made us a much easier target. Worse yet, the Germans had all the eighty-eights in the world, it seemed, and they were shooting at us with all of them.

We were at twelve thousand feet when we heard a kind of metallic *ka-whump,* like when you clap down on still water with a cupped hand to make a little geyser, only on a huge scale. It shook the ship, hard. I wasn't scared at first, because the concussion stunned me. Then I looked out the window to see if the propellers were all turning, and just then something hit the right wing, *wham!* The wing collapsed and I thought, "Uh oh. We're in trouble." I felt Felgar drop us out of the formation, to reduce the danger to the other planes of us blowing up. That's when I got scared. I seriously wondered if we were going to make it.

Then a flak shell hit the nose of the ship. A lot of what happened now I didn't see, but pieced together from other guys later—from Swinger, Fox, and Moellering, and Wiley and Homer after we were captured, and from Felgar several months later, soon before returning to the States—so this is it the best I can make out. You have to keep in mind that everything that happened happened in a matter of seconds, and all at once. It was chaos.

Anyway, the shell that hit the nose knocked out all the plexiglass and the instrument panel and took off two of Felgar's fingers. A piece of shrapnel hit him in the forehead and knocked him out. I didn't know any of that at the time—I just figured something was really amiss because we didn't have a chance in hell to make it and I was waiting for Felgar to ring the bailout bell, the signal that we were to jump, and it wasn't ringing.

Right behind the pilot there was this little opening that the pilots entered and exited the plane through, but it was small. Real tight. And the pilots had their parachutes on, on their backs. Benitez, the rookie copilot, tried to get out through that opening to bail out, but his parachute got snagged, so Chase, the engineer, tried to help him—he actually stood on Benitez's shoulders to push him through.

Then there was an explosion that blew off the tail assembly, and the plane was going down spinning in a circle. That was when Felgar woke up, which we figured because the bailout bell rang and he had to be the guy who set it off.

Well, I always had the chutes ready in case something like this happened, so I could lay my hands on them. I threw one to Moellering, the radioman, who'd come out from his little desk. Bob Fox, the tail gunner, had managed to crawl almost to the plane's waist before the tail got blown off, but got stuck at one point and I pulled him the rest of the way and handed him a chute. Later Swinger told me that *he* got stuck and I helped him get out of the ball-turret, though I don't remember that, but I do remember giving him his chute.

I don't know exactly when, in all of this—like I said, it was chaos, so much happening at once—but I managed to get my own chute on. You hooked the chute to a harness that you wore, and those harnesses were god-awful uncomfortable, cinching you up at the crotch and pulling you over into a stoop, like an old man. You could hardly walk. So we loosened them up, but that made hooking up the chutes more difficult because the straps were loose. And we'd never hooked our chutes up before. So we were trying to figure out how to hook the parachutes up at the same time that we were going to be using them and were in a state of near-panic.

When Swinger got his chute on he went to the rear escape door, the door down near the floor where we got on the plane and off. He unlocked it and tried to open it, but it wouldn't open, so he found a handhold over the door and hung on to it while frantically kicking the door with both feet. Finally the door popped and flew open and then he was hanging in that space where the door had been, but he didn't release his grip to bail out. Paralyzed, I guess. So he was hanging there and I was on my hands and knees and beating him on the head and hollering,

"Swinger! Drop! Drop! Let go!"

But instead of letting go, he somehow or other—I don't know how the hell he did it—he crawled back up into the airplane and said, "Carl, you go first."

And I said, "Then get the hell out of the way!" I pushed him aside and bailed out, and the three guys followed me, Bob Fox, Moellering, and Swinger. Because our harnesses were loose, when our chutes opened we got a terrific, unforgettable jolt right in the crotch. As we were floating down I looked up at the plane, to see what was happening. I didn't see them, but Homer and Wiley, the navigator and the bombardier, were standing in the bomb bay about to jump. Benitez and Chase, the copilot and engineer, managed to get out of that tight little opening. I saw them emerge and pull the ripcords and their chutes open. But Felgar was still in the plane, which was going down spinning. It was obvious that the centrifugal force was pinning him in. Unless he was dead.

Just then the plane, or what was left of it, exploded again and turned into a huge fire ball. I was astonished. I didn't think there was enough left—enough gas, enough plane—*to* explode, and wondered what it was that ignited. I saw the flames consume Benitez's and Chase's parachutes, and watched them plummet straight down. I felt real bad about that, but especially for that West Point kid. I regarded him as a kid even though he was older than me. First mission. A helluva way to die, for both of them.

Meanwhile, Swinger woke up in mid-air, and his chute was open, though he didn't remember pulling the rip cord or anything. He saw that his arms and legs were all burned and he passed out again, in mid-air.

I found out later that that explosion blew Wiley and Homer out of the bomb bay—they came right out of that fireball, miraculously, you have to say. It had also knocked them out. When they came to they saw that their chutes were open, somehow—they wondered if the blast ripped them open—but when they saw the shape they were in—their clothes all burned, their faces, the skin on their legs—*wham!* they also passed out again. Later they said they didn't remember hitting the ground.

Just as miraculously, that explosion also blew Felgar out, and he managed to get his chute open. I later found out that he hit the ground hard near a little creek. The Germans came and got him. He had a real bad cut on his forehead, and he had pieces of flak shrapnel in his body plus the two fingers missing.

One thing you need to know is that in training they taught us nothing about parachutes. Here we'd had drills in hand-to-hand combat, infantry crawling, water survival, but *no* instruction in parachuting except to pull the rip-cord. They didn't even say *when* we should pull it, to count to three or five first to make sure we had cleared the plane. We never had a practice jump. We'd never even *looked* at a chute. And it cost us a couple of lives. When Benitez and Chase got free of the plane, they immediately pulled their rip cords; if they had waited a few seconds, they would have been far enough from the plane that their chutes wouldn't have caught fire.

Anyway, as I was floating down, I looked up and said, "God damn, there's holes in my chute," and then I looked down at the ground and saw German soldiers down there with rifles. They were shooting at us as we were coming down. I could hear the bullets whizzing by, could hear them tearing more holes in my chute, and I said to myself, "Damn, those guys are shooting at us, and they mean business!" I remembered this paratrooper telling me once, "If you want to go to the left, you pull on the cords on your right and you'll tilt the chute and start going left; if you want to go right, pull on the left cords and you'll go right." So I started pulling the cords to go away from them. They started chasing after me—I could hear them yelling.

There were some French people trimming the trees in a little orchard. I aimed for that little orchard, and somehow or other I made it, but then crashed through some trees and wound up on my back with broken tree limbs all over me. I scrambled to get out from under the debris, and next thing I knew, I was looking at the muzzle of a rifle. Then I saw a German soldier holding it, and heard him say, "For you, ze vore iss ofer."

PART 3 – POW

Well, for me the war might be over, but I wouldn't be going home. Only a couple of missions to go and here I was in in the countryside of France in the hands of German soldiers. SS, no less, the worst of the worst. I was so ticked off. But I was also thankful to be alive.

They took me back to the road they were retreating on, the one we'd been bombing where we got hit. One of them asked me, *"Was ist die Namen?"* What is your name?

I said, "Carl Weller."

"Carl *Veller*? Why do you fight your own people?"

I said, "I'm fighting *for* my own people."

He gave me a dirty look. I was lucky he didn't kill me right on the spot, for backtalk. Sometimes the SS shot guys for less. But I was nineteen. A kid. I didn't know enough to keep my trap shut.

The Germans picked several of us up and put us in this little vehicle that looked like a Jeep. There was a guard and another guy driving. He started driving down this little country road—not the one they were retreating on—one lane, with trees and hedgerows on both sides of the road. We were sitting in the Jeep going down that road and the guard says to me, *"Flieger, Flieger,"* and he's pointing at the sky, meaning "Watch out for airplanes" because there were P-38's and P51's all over the place.

Well, in about five minutes, sure enough, I saw a couple of P-51's. I tapped the driver on the back and pointed up at the sky and said, *"Flieger, Flieger!"* Like that cabbie in London, he stopped the vehicle immediately, only this time we all jumped out and ran for cover in the hedgerows. This P-51 came down, shot at our vehicle with tracer bullets to get a line on it, then he fired off a rocket that hit it dead on and blew it all to hell. That was what is now called "friendly fire." Even though we knew the pilot didn't know who we were, and even though he was on our side, it still didn't feel very friendly, I can tell you that.

When the planes had flown away, the driver came out from the hedgerow, looked at what was left of the vehicle, and said, "Und now ve valk." And walk we did.

Marching in France at that time was most dangerous. Like I said, there were fighter planes, British and American, all over the place, bombing and strafing the Germans wherever they saw them. And we prisoners were retreating with the Germans. And the pilots couldn't tell us apart.

We finally got to an encampment behind the front lines of a battle that was going on where they held us for about three days. The encampment was on a farm close by some railroad tracks. They just set us down and we stayed right where we were. There were some seventy-five, eighty German soldiers there, so they could keep close watch over us.

Some of them made a display of two American flying suits, waving them sort of like flags. The guard beside me said they were the suits of two men from our plane. Benitez and Chase. I don't know what they were doing with those suits. They had taken them off their bodies for trophies or souvenirs, I guess.

On this flat-bed railroad car there was an eighty-eight millimeter anti-air-craft gun, and a big German next to it was waving at me, waving and waving and waving. I was about twenty or thirty yards away from him. I looked at the guard beside me, gesturing that I didn't understand, and he said, "That's the guy who shot your airplane down." The big guy was still waving like crazy, so I gave him a little salute. I didn't know if that was the thing to do—still don't—but I can say he looked real pleased.

We were quite close to the battle line. We could hear the artillery fire—cannon firing, shells going off. For some reason they took Swinger and put him in what kind of looked like a bomb shelter that was dug in the ground. I think it had been used by the people living on the farm as a root cellar or something like that. It was half full of water—water up to his hips—and they left him in there all night, and the next day and night. When he came out he was a nervous wreck, and I didn't blame him. It was one hell of an uncomfortable spot.

After three days they still hadn't given us anything to eat. Some women from a neighboring farm came. They had made some sandwiches they wanted to give us. The Germans told them no, they couldn't give us anything, and told them to go back home where they belonged. I will say the Germans didn't take these sandwiches for themselves, which they could have, of course, but even so...

A couple of hours later these women came back with the sandwiches. They argued with the German soldiers—I have to give them credit, they stood right up to those guys—and they finally persuaded the Germans to let us have the sandwiches they had made for us. And there were some cookies and cake in there too. We thanked those women profusely. It was one of the best meals I have ever had in my life.

The next day we got up and there was a big trailer there. You could hear pigs squealing in it. Apparently they had taken the pigs from one of the farms in the area. They decided they were going to cook one of them up for the troops. They strung it up with ropes between a couple of trees, dressed it out, and were about to start a fire underneath it when they noticed it was quite hairy, so they decided to remove the hair before they cooked it. They took a blow torch, burned all the hair on the animal and brushed it off with their bayonets, like brushing lint off a wool suit with a butcher knife. Then they started a fire underneath it and cooked it there for hours and hours and hours. They cooked it until the next day, when they made it into a kind of stew. They gave us prisoners a bowl of it, and all you could taste was hair—burnt hair. Which tastes the same as it smells—real bad. We were so hungry we ate it anyway, but we didn't pay any compliments to the chefs.

Later on that day they put us on another truck. We sat in the back, on benches on each side. We came to a spot where there were a lot of German soldiers milling around and stopped for a break. The Germans used to carry a little canister on their belt, and this one German reached into his canister and brought out a piece of sausage. Looking at us, he cut a piece of that sausage off, ate it, and put the rest of it back into his canister. That stuck in our craws I can tell you. But it was hard for us to know what they were eating day by day because we didn't exactly break bread together, you know? But they did give us some black bread. We all took a bite and threw it away. Tasted like crud. Months later, on our

long march west at the end of the war, when we were

really hungry, we would have loved it.

While we were sitting there, a German soldier, an

older guy, on the other side of the road, motioned for me

to come over. He wanted to talk to me. I shook my head

no because I was afraid to, afraid the guards might think I

was trying to make a break for it or something. They

were drinking, they were SS, they were losing the war,

and I didn't want to give them a reason or an excuse to

shoot me. But he kept gesturing, real urgently, so, scared

though I was, I finally let myself down off the truck and

walked over to him.

He gestured for me to sit down beside him.   We

were sitting on the ground. He pulled out a bottle of

Schnapps and offered me a drink, which I accepted and

enjoyed, then he started talking to me. *"Alles ist kaputt,"* he said. I asked what he meant, as best I could since I spoke no German, and he answered as best he could, since he spoke no English. What he managed to tell me was that he had lost almost his whole family—his wife, his sons, his daughters, his mother, his father, his grand-father. The only one left was his youngest son, and he was on his way to the Russian front, which meant that soon he, the man talking to me, he would be the only one left in his whole family. It was sad. He kept saying, *"Alles ist kaputt. Alles ist kaputt,"* and for him it was no exaggeration. I told him I was sorry, and I was. He had nothing left, poor guy. Nothing. Made me feel almost lucky.

I didn't understand why he wanted to share his sad news with me, and his sense of defeat—his despair, really—but I guessed that he had to share it with some-one and he couldn't with his German comrades—the SS were so fanatical they might execute him for treason. Sharing it with an American was safe. But why he singled me out I didn't know, so I asked. He explained that I looked like his youngest son, the one who was on his way to his death.

From that place they took us to a small prison camp near Wetzlar. We traveled mostly at night, by the way—there were so many fighters flying around, British and American, that traveling by day was almost suicidal. Anyway, in that camp they had interrogation officers, and the one who interrogated me asked,

"Was ist die namen?"

I said, "Carl Weller" and gave him my serial number.

He asked me some more questions—what outfit I was with, what position I held, what missions I had flown, etc. etc.—and over and over I said, "I'm sorry, but I can't answer that question. I can only give you my name and serial number."

Finally he said to me, "Carl Veller. Why do you fight your own people?" Like that other guy who asked me the same question. Only this time I said nothing in reply. Then this guy said, "Actually we don't have to ask you any questions. We know all about you."

He went to a file cabinet—the place was full of file cabinets—and got a piece of paper out of one of the files, looked it over and told me the name of the street I lived on in Detroit. He told me where I went to school, and my father's name and occupation, and my mother's name, stuff like that. He said, "We know more about you than you know about yourself." And I think he well may have.

This was before the internet! I had no idea—and still have no idea!—how they had all this information, right at fingertip no less, but they did. Kind of scary, that degree of thoroughness. And so German!

He turned me loose. There was a barracks across the street from where he did his work. Bob Fox and Swinger and the radioman, Moellering, and me—the four of us got put in this barracks across the road with about thirty infantry guys who'd also been taken prisoner. We got to talking with them, getting acquainted—you know, sharing our stories, the differences between being taken as a flyboy and as a grunt. And the similarities.

When it got dark we got in these bunk beds that didn't have mattresses, just the boards on the bottom, and some of the boards were missing, so we knew it was going to be really hard to get any sleep. And we knew it wouldn't do any good to complain, so we kept our complaints to ourselves.

Well into the night we could hear a commotion going on outside. At dark the Germans had put shutters on all the windows, but they weren't all that tight—there were cracks you could look through and see what was going on outside, so we took a look. There were a lot of German guards out there, twenty-five or thirty of them, drinking. Next thing we saw, some of them were setting up a machine gun on a stand. After they got it set up, one of them busted into the barracks hollering, *"Wo ist die fier Luftwaffe?"* Where are the four air corps guys?

There was a fellow there named Gertz, an infantryman I'd been talking to who was from Hamtramck, a town a little north of Detroit. Turned out he had a German background, could even speak it. When the German asked where the Luftwaffe were, Gertz pointed at the four of us, Fox, Swinger, Moellering, and me. I don't think he knew they had set up that machine gun. For some reason the German singled me out—came over to me—I was in a top bunk—put a flashlight in my face and a Luger in my ear, and started hollering, *"Herauskommen, raus!"* Get out of here—get out there!

I said, "I'm not getting out of here." He shook me and shook me and kept hollering at me, but I hardly knew any German, so I decided to see if he knew any English and said, "If you think I'm gonna go out there and let you execute me, you're crazy. I'm not going to do that. I'm going to stay right here."

He tried to pull me out, but I wasn't having any of it. After a while he gave up and went back outside and talked to the guys with the machine gun, then busted back in and shook me and hollered at me to go out there, and again I said absolutely not, I wasn't going to go get gunned down. Then he started yelling, "If all four of the Luftwaffe guys don't go out, we're going to shoot everybody in the barracks! We'll shoot through the walls and we'll kill everybody!"

Some of the infantry guys were saying, "You all go on out—you better go out! Otherwise they're going to kill us all." So now us air corps guys had the Germans against us and the American infantry against us.

We said, "Hell no! We're not going to do that." Then I said to Gertz, "Look, when you fingered us you didn't realize the Germans have a machine gun set up out there, and they're drunk as hell and wanting to shoot us Air Corps guys. For bombing them. They mean business. We're not going to give ourselves up. We're not going to walk out there and let them execute us. You're the only one of us who can speak German, so it's up to you to talk to them, cool them off a little bit."

Gertz said, "Okay, I'll do the best I can," and started talking to the guy, who was obviously drunk. They sat down and talked for hours. Every once in a while the German would get up, go outside, talk to the guys there, then come back in hollering threats again, and Gertz would cool him off. I don't know what time it was, three or four in the morning—this whole thing had been going on for hours—and the guard had started sobering up and reconsidering, I guess, because he went back out and they finally packed up the machine gun and left. But after all that commotion and stress, and having boards for a mattress, I don't think I slept an hour.

I give Gertz a lot of credit. At first, when he pointed us out, I thought he might be a rat, but he stood up to this guy and talked him out of shooting anybody.

In the morning some of the guys talked to the German commander of that particular barracks, or got word to him somehow or other, because next thing we knew he dressed those soldiers who'd threatened us down, especially the one who came into the barracks hollering at us.

On the way to the camp we were bombed a couple of times. Once there were quite a few of us American POW's in this pottery manufacturing plant, where they made dishes and cups and saucers, only there wasn't hardly anything left of this building, it had been bombed so many times, but the Americans came back dropping hundred pound bombs, small bombs, personnel bombs, so they must have seen all those people down there and figured to take them out, not realizing those people were Americans. Us. We took cover and luckily no one got hurt.

Another time they put us in the cellar of a house for the night. An old-fashioned cellar, dark and dank, with stone walls, a dirt floor. *But,* it was a wine cellar! Various varieties of wine, cider, champagne. The warned us not to drink the champagne, but they might as well have saved their breath. There was no way we *weren't* going to sample some champagne, along with the wine and cider. When the guards heard the champagne corks pop, they would come down and say, "*Was ist los?*" What's going on? And we would say, "*Nichts! Alles ist gut.*" And all *was* good. *Very* good. A great night, one of the few that we *didn't* want to escape.

One time I was by myself—I can't remember exactly where I was, and I can't remember how, but I was by myself, and it was a beautiful day, the sun shining, the air warm, and I decided to catch a few rays. All of a sudden I heard this engine, and I looked around, and from behind this building a Hurricane or a Spitfire, I'm not sure which, only that it was British, it shot out, flying real low, and he was looking for me, to shoot me. When I saw him he had seen me and had leveled off. I rolled over behind this concrete barrier just as he let loose with his machine guns. He didn't know I was an American, of course. He raked the hell out of the ground where I had just been sitting—he had a line on me for sure. I heard him just in time.

They loaded us all up on a truck and we went through Wetzlar. People were gathered in the town, and they were throwing rocks at us, bottles, anything they could get their hands on. Not at the infantry guys, but at us fliers. We finally figured it out: we had 8th Air Corps patches on our shirts. We were in Germany now, and we were the guys who had been bombing them, and they were retaliating, getting even the best they could. The same as the guards who wanted to shoot us. So we ripped the patches off. That made it a little bit better.

We wound up in Frankfurt. They let us off at a railroad yard, where they walked us past a string of railroad cars, passenger cars—the kind people travel in, not freight—that were full of dead people. Full of them. People of all ages, old people and children. Looked like mostly old people. The cars had been shot up quite badly. Nobody was moving in them. And there were two soldiers hanging from a lamp post. Hung by the neck. Somebody said they were Canadian. I think the Germans wanted to scare us with this sight. It *was* frightening, for sure, but not frightening so much as just awful. We passed the dead people in the railroad cars and the soldiers hanging from the lamp post, then we were put in box cars. There were other POW's they brought there, and they put us all in box cars, to take us to a prison camp, we figured. Then they locked the doors—we couldn't get out.

The box car I was in had one little window—an aperture, I guess you should call it, since it had no glass—that was the only source of air in the car. It was about ten inches by seven inches, something like that, and it had barbed wire strung all over it, so no one could squeeze out. I doubt if anyone could have anyway, it was so small, but the barbed wire made it absolutely impossible. The car was so crowded you couldn't lay down. The best you could do was sit down and fold your legs up, more or less, sort of like a ball-turret gunner.

Well, right after they shut and locked the door, one of the POW's went berserk. Hollering and screaming that he had to get out, trying to pull the barbed wire out of the window, and cutting his hands all up. A bunch of guys pulled him off the window and subdued him by force, which wasn't easy, the way he was thrashing around. They finally calmed him down—I think maybe *stilled* him is the word—but seeing someone lose it like that scared me more than the situation itself. Or the dead people. I guess I was afraid *I* might go nuts like that.

We were gone twenty minutes, thirty minutes, something like that—we put this whole thing together afterwards, because at the time we couldn't see anything—but anyway, some P-51's spotted us. The railroad cars weren't marked, we knew that. They were supposed to be, like with POWS and RED CROSS written on the roof, so pilots could tell friend from foe, but the Germans didn't want them to be able to tell friend from foe, so the P-51 pilots had no idea there were Americans in these box cars. They came down and made a couple of passes and shot up the train pretty bad. We came to a stop.

Being locked up like that, we had no idea how many people were injured, how many killed by all this action. After the 51's left, the Germans opened up some of the box cars and we got out. There was a guy there I'll never forget. He was about six foot five, real athletic, wearing an American uniform, and he was hollering at the Germans, really raising hell with them, and he wouldn't shut up. He was three or four cars ahead of us. I didn't know who he was, what his deal was—no one seemed to know him. I don't know what happened to him—far as I know they put him back in the car. I was surprised they didn't shoot him. So many things happened and didn't happen arbitrarily. A lot of craziness in war.

I saw that the Germans had detached the engine and run it off into a tunnel, where it couldn't be shot up. They brought it out and loaded us all back into the cars. Our car hadn't got hit—we were lucky. I understand a couple of guys got killed—I wouldn't swear to it. I didn't see it. They hooked the engine back up and we were on our way again.

Our next stop was Stalag Luft IV, the prison camp for airmen (*Luft* means air in German) near Pomerania, which was east of Dresden almost on the Polish border. In fact, it now *is* in Poland, I think. Deep in eastern Germany, near the Baltic Sea. By now we had more guys, God only knows how many and how they got captured. There was a train load of us. We stopped at a little station, got out of the box cars, and walked to the prison camp, about four miles.

The camp was huge—hundreds of barracks holding nine, ten thousand men. Once we were in it we each got a Red Cross food parcel and were taken to a building with a lot of showers in it. They took our parcels and put them on a table—more like a counter you see in a store. They had us take off all our clothes and rummaged through them, to see if we had anything con-cealed in them. They looked into every orifice of our body to make sure we weren't hiding something *there*—I don't know what they thought they might find—then they put us in the shower. When we finished our showers we put our clothes back on, the same ones we had been wearing for who knows how long, and went back to the table.

The guards ripped off a big sheet of butcher paper and laid it over the table, then opened the parcels up and poured everything in them, all the food, out on the paper —Spam, powdered milk, instant coffee, jam, chocolate— all together on the paper. And you have to understand, much as you may not like Spam and powdered milk—and I don't myself, nowadays—to a hungry POW they were like *haut cuisine.* Then this guard who'd been ordering us around, he took his bayonet and mixed it all up, as if he was looking for something contraband. I was getting hotter by the minute, because I figured (and I was right!) that that was the only decent food we were going to be getting for quite a while, and for all we knew maybe the only food. After he got it all mixed up real good, he wrapped it all up in the paper, in a big heap, and said, *"Raus!"*

So I "roused" and walked away. Then I heard him hollering at me. You know, he wanted me to stop. And I thought, "To hell with you" and kept on going. I was heading for the door and he came up behind me. I had hair in those days. He grabbed me by it and dragged me all the way back to that table, took the package and hit me right in the stomach with it, and said, *"Now raus!"* He wanted me to take the package and throw it in the trash. I was so mad, because he'd destroyed all the food in it, that I wasn't going to listen to any of his stuff and walked out.

Turned out that that guard was called Big Stoop, and he was the bully of the camp, riding POW's and working them over all the time, and there was nothing you could do about it. After that one encounter I steered clear of him. As far as I was concerned, the less trouble the better.

Then we were taken to our barracks. The barracks were wood structures, maybe twenty-five by seventy feet, and three feet off the ground. Insulation? You've got to be kidding. Landscaping? Forget it. These were bare bone structures, dozens and dozens of them, *hundreds* of them in rows in a bare bones compound. We were assigned a building to go to, and a room in it, and that was where we were going to be living for a while, more or less. Depends on your definition of living.

There were about forty guys per room. When we got there, the guys who were there already asked if the Germans had made us run that four miles from the box cars to the camp, if they had beat us and stabbed us in the butt along the way. We said no, then they told us that that's what they did to the group that arrived right before we did, worked them over with clubs and bayonets and dogs the whole four miles. We said no and wondered why they didn't, and also why they did to that one group. So arbitrary. But that's the way it is in war.

There was only one window in our room, a small window. The bunk beds, instead of two high, were three high, to accommodate three people per bed site instead of two. They'd been made on the spot there, with rough lumber. They didn't have any mattresses, so what they did, they gave us each a paper bag that was about six feet long and twenty-four inches wide. They brought in bales of hay, straw, and you stuffed the straw into this paper bag until you got it to where you could sleep on it, you hoped. That was our mattress, which in time got real moldy. We were issued one blanket. At night you laid down on your paper bag mattress and covered yourself with your one blanket. We slept in our clothes.

Even with three tiered bunks they still didn't have beds for everyone, so those without a bed had to sleep underneath the bottom bunk, on the floor. That's what I got. Three guys on top of me, floor, then crawl space underneath. The guys who were there already told me, "You can sleep on the table instead."

The table they pointed at was the table everyone ate on, about six, seven feet long. "No," I said, "I'll sleep under the bunks, thanks." That way I couldn't fall off.

And that was where I slept for the duration, on the floor, which was really cold, much colder than the bunks, because the air from outside came up right through the cracks in the floor. And I had so little room that I had to sleep either on my back or on my stomach the whole night through, because there wasn't room to turn over. I usually slept on my back, but was always afraid I might get peed on, since you couldn't get up in the middle of the night to go to the john, which was in another building and we were locked in for the night.

When you got to the camp, besides the paper bag and straw, they gave you a spoon and a fork. Early in the morning they blew a horn to wake you up. You'd send a couple of men over to the building where they did the so-called cooking, and they would pick up a container with ersatz tea. There wasn't any coffee. Every once in a while they'd give you some bread. They wouldn't give each of us a loaf of bread—oh hell no—they'd give us one loaf for eight or ten people. This bread was black, like the bread we got soon after we were captured, but it wasn't the same. When you cut this bread open—and it was so hard you wished you had a hatchet or a saw—you could look down into it and see like a little line of gum, something that had settled down to the bottom.

One of the main ingredients was, I believe, sawdust. Another was weevils. Not much nutrition to it. So we'd cut the bread up—and boy, you had to be real careful not to cut any one piece bigger than another—then pass it out, one piece per guy. And we ate it. Even though, as I said, it was filled with sawdust and weevils. Beggars can't be choosers, you know.

No such thing as eggs or bacon or waffles or Wheaties or anything like that—nothing tasty or nourishing.

There was no lunch. Around five o'clock, if we got anything to eat at all, we'd get a cup of rutabaga soup. Rutabagas were like a cross between a turnip and a head of cabbage. Some of them were bigger than your head—huge big things—and like the bread, they were almost like wood. The Germans would boil them for a while and that was the soup. *Soup du jour,* literally, the only thing we got for dinner.

I used to dream about food. Fried chicken my mother used to make. Mashed potatoes and biscuits and gravy. We all did. It seemed like every night when we went to bed some of the guys—the newer ones, usually—would say, "My mother made the best this or that." They would go on for a while like that—remember, many of them if not most were still teenagers—until some of the veterans of the place would say, "Ah, shut up, you guys! Quit talking about food so we can sleep!"

The windows of the barracks all had shutters which the guards would close at night or early evening and fasten them shut. Then the guards would walk around the perimeters of the buildings, each with a dog, and the dogs would go underneath to make sure there wasn't anybody there. Some of the rooms had little potbelly stoves in them. It was cold then, starting to get cold. What the prisoners would do, they'd move the stoves over a few feet and cut a hole in the floor underneath the stove, so they could crawl out and try to escape that way, hoping they wouldn't be detected by the dogs. I have no idea how they cut the hole, or if anyone ever managed to escape that way. We didn't have a stove in our barracks.

In the morning there was a roll call. It wasn't a roll call exactly, where they would call everyone by name. They would just count us. We'd go out in the yard and form up in lines of five that were four deep, and they would count the lines. And guys would do crazy things. They'd stoop down so they couldn't be seen, and they would move around so there'd be five in one line and three in another. Things like that to tick off the Germans, who liked everything to be in order and accounted for, so they'd have to start counting all over again. Then the Major, I think it was, the guy in charge of the camp, he'd come out with his long leather coat on and high shiny boots—they really had beautiful uniforms, I have to say—and read us the riot act. This happened every morning and every evening, every day.

At the corners of the camp they had machine gun towers with guards on duty twenty-four seven. We could walk around the camp, but there were stakes in the ground with a wire running on top of them about six feet from the main fence topped with barbed wire, and that space in between there was filled with tangle wire. That space was *verboten*. If you stepped over that line, or if you even stumbled or fell across it, they could shoot you right on the spot. And if they didn't shoot you, you were still all tangled up in that barbed wire. So we were pretty well contained.

The johns were all in a long narrow building separate from the barracks, a gigantic privy, hole after hole in wood planks perched over a deep pit in the dirt. Given the fencing and the guards, to escape you pretty much had to dig a tunnel, which from underneath the barracks was well-nigh impossible since they had those dogs. The safest way was to dig one starting from the outhouse pit—the pit full of the waste of hundreds of men—and some guys actually did. I don't know if any actually succeeded, but I heard about one group of guys who dug as far as half way to the fence, then it rained for three straight days and their tunnel caved in.

There *were* a couple of guys who attempted a surface-escape, I guess you could call it. Seems they got a wire cutter somehow—we figured they bribed some guards—and they managed to cut through the tangle wire and underneath the guard tower and through the perimeter fence without being seen by man or dog, which made us think there had to be a set-up, but as soon as they got through the fence the guards in the tower opened up on them, killing one and wounding the other. We saw the guards bring the bodies in—they were letting us know what happens to those who try to escape. The wounded fellow died soon after. Oh it was a set-up alright.

The camp didn't have showers or anything like that. You could go behind the barracks where there was a water faucet, and put some water in a bucket and give yourself a sponge bath. That was as close as you could come to getting clean. The only clothes you had was what you were wearing, and if you wanted to wash them, you had do it out of a bucket of water, but then you had to dry them. And you had to have something on—it was cold—but like I said, we had only the clothes on our backs Bottom line: we were dirty.

After the morning count we were pretty much on our own. Not that there was much to do. We used to walk the wire, as we put it, walking around the camp. Guys would get together and wonder how soon the war was going to be over. When the Battle of the Bulge happened, and the Germans put a serious dent in the Americans' advance, the guards got real cocky. They thought it was going to be another Dunkirk, where all the British were forced out of France at the beginning of the war. So they were hot there for a while, but then Patton came in and kicked their ass.

We talked a lot, of course, and there were always all kinds of rumors floating around. Like the Germans were going to take all the POW's, regardless of what nationality they were, up to Berchtesgaden, which was where Hitler's mountain retreat was, and surround him with all these POW's so the Allies wouldn't bomb him. Or he was going to have all of us POW's executed before the Allies rescued us. Or he was going to surrender to the Americans so he wouldn't have to face the Russians. All kinds of stuff like that.

The new POW's would sit around and say, "Let me tell you how I got shot down," and the guys who'd been there for a while would say, "Aw shut up! We've heard all the bailout stories we want to hear." All that the guys who'd been there a while wanted to know was what was going on back home. Homesick is hardly the word for how POWS's felt.

One day they brought a bunch of new guys in, and I asked this one guy, "What kind of music are they playing nowadays?" I was always curious about the music back home. He said, "I don't know much about it, but there's this one song they're playing a lot, called 'I'll Walk Alone.'" And he sang it. It was about the loneliness of the ones on the home front as well as the ones overseas, the loneliness of both missing each other. A real downer, in a way, but we could all relate to it.

There were other downers. Bad news in letters. Dear John letters. One guy's fiancée wrote something like, "Darling, you were missing a month so I got married." The "darling" part was funny, but bitter-funny, you know? Another one that was bitter-funny said something like, "I'm glad you liked the sweater, but I'd rather a fighting man got it." You just couldn't believe it.

Sometimes there were lines that were simply funny. A couple I remember word for word. "I'm glad you went down before flying became dangerous." We wondered if the folks back home had any idea. We even wondered if they were brain-damaged. The best of them all, the one that cracked us all up the most, said, "I hope you're not drinking too much." And we were all saying, "Jesus, I wish I *could* drink too much!"

Sometimes there were football games, the British against the Americans. It wasn't exactly American football, but you could run with the ball—it was Rugby, basically. They played hard. In one big game a couple of guys got injured—a broken arm, a broken leg. The German then put an end to the football games. They didn't want to be bothered with taking care of injuries, I guess.

We had a variety of POWS' in there: British soldiers, Canadian soldiers, free French. I think there were even some Australians, in addition to us Americans. It was really an interesting place.

We had English prisoners there who'd been captured when the English were trying to get out of France and back home to England, using any and every kind of boat they could muster—anything that would float. Dunkirk. Some of the English didn't make it, of course, and got captured at Dunkirk and put in prison camp. This was at the very beginning of the war, long before we were in it—in 1940, around the end of May, the beginning of June. So these guys had been prisoners for a long long time. Poor guys, the diet they were on for so long—five, six years—the diet had ruined their stomachs. They all had ulcers, it seemed. Well, in our

Red Cross food parcels we used to get powdered milk,

and we'd give it to the Brits, and maybe they'd give us

some cigarettes or something in return, because the pow-

dered milk was the one thing they could keep in their

stomachs, that could keep them going. Often we just

gave them our milk.

They were very clever, those Brits. One fellow

even made a clock out of tin cans. How he ever cut those

cans up and put them together like that I have no idea. I

looked at it and it was the most amazing thing I ever saw.

We had Free French people in there, pilots. Some

of the pilots, like British pilots, were not officers; they

were sergeants, a lot of them. So they were in the same

prison camp I was in instead of the camps for officers.

All the American pilots and copilots and bombardiers

and navigators were lieutenants, and they went to a

separate camp. I can't say what those camps were like because I was never in one.

In addition to food parcels, the Red Cross also brought in some baseballs and bats we could play with. They even managed to bring in some instruments. We had this little piano keyboard in the barracks, and we had guys who could sing and tell jokes, things like that, so once in a while we put on little shows. Now, at six or seven o'clock the Germans would close all the doors, bolt them so you couldn't get in or out, so the guys who came from other barracks to see the show had to get there before the barracks were closed, and after the show they had to sleep overnight in the hall, which ran down the entire length of the building. A slumber party of sorts, if you will. That's where we put the shows on, in the hall.

Being the comedian on the plane, I decided to play in a couple of the shows in the camp. There used to be a comedian on the radio whose name was Al Pearce.

He did a character he called Elmer Blurt, a very nervous

insecure door-to-door salesman who had a line he said all

the time that became a national catch phrase: "Nobody at

home, I hope, I hope, I hope."

So I did a skit as Elmer Blurt selling life insur-

ance that had the motto, "You get the money as soon as

you die." I knocked on a door saying "Nobody's at home,

I hope, I hope, I hope," but from behind the door a

woman asked,

"Who is it?"

"A life insurance salesman," I said.

She said, "I can't come to the door—I'm not

dressed!"

And I said, "That's alright, ma'am: our policies

cover everything." That sort of thing.

The gag that brought down the house, though, was when I offered her a life insurance policy for all the dictators. "When they die, who's the beneficiary?" she asked,

and I answered, *"Everybody."*

Pearce used a high-pitched falsetto voice for a character he called "Tizzie Lish." I thought it might be fun to do Tizzie too, dressed up like a woman, especially since she was proverbially ugly. So some buddies wrapped a German flag around me for a dress, put a mop on my head for hair, put lipstick and rouge on me—they had a regular make-up guy working on me. We got the make-up from the Red Cross, which sounds crazy, make-up for men, but so it was. We had a guy who played trumpet, and he even got a trumpet from the Red Cross. So there I was, all lipsticked and rouged up, and I came out saying in a falsetto,

"Hello, folksies. This is your body beautiful, Tizzie Lish, the soda pop girl. You know why they call me the soda pop girl? Because I go for any guy from seven up!... I was on the bus the other day, and this fellow said I looked like Betty Grable, and I said, "Have you ever seen Betty Grable?" And he says, "No, that's what I mean. You look like something I've never seen before."

Lizzie Tish always had a recipe, so we cooked one up ourselves. "Now boys, Halloween is coming up, so we've got a special Halloween recipe for you. You go down to your corner grocery store and get yourself a pound of wienies and bring them back to your kitchen. Now, you know at the end of the wienie there's a little piece of string? Take that string off. Don't throw it away! Take that string off and take all the meat out of the casing, then blow the casing up and take that string and re-tie it so the air can't get out. Then, when company comes for dinner and they take a fork and stick it in that wienie, and all the air escapes, you say, "Happy Hollow Wienie!"

A joke so bad it got a big laugh.

I also sang a song, "The Nearness of You," a real romantic song where I sang that the only thing that turned me on (as we say nowadays) was not the moon or sweet talk or soft lights, but the nearness of *you,* pointing at the guys in the audience. Well, I schmaltzed it up for all it was worth, like an over-the-top, lovey-dovey, very horny Rita Hayworth, with as many appropriate, or maybe I should say inappropriate, gestures as I could.

Everything we did in those shows was silly and fun and upbeat. We didn't need any blues. "I'll walk alone" was enough.

Another of our diversions, we pooled all our raisins from the Red Cross parcels, put them in water, and let them ferment, so we could have raisin wine for Christmas. But we figured out another use for it besides our own consumption. There was a Polish guy who came into the camp periodically with a horse-drawn tank to clean out the privies. The tank had a motor which he started with a gas-soaked torch, and attached to the tank was a big hose that he sucked out all the waste with—a nasty job for sure, and one that the Germans had a Polish guy do because they didn't want to do it themselves. Well, around Christmas time the wine was ready, and we gave some to the Polish guy. More than some, actually. We got him drunk (and we were pretty lit ourselves), then when he wasn't operating at full capacity, I guess you could say, we unhitched his horse from the wagon and took turns riding it. A whole lotta fun, I have to say, till the Germans decided it was too much fun and stopped it.

There were things going on in the barracks that the Germans didn't and couldn't know about. One of them was a radio. A radio that we could reach the BBC with. So every night we got the news. Just before they closed the barracks for the night, some guards would come in and shutter the windows, then leave and lock the door. But there were cracks you could see through, and we'd post lookouts and listen to the news. We'd find out how Patton was doing, and all the different generals. At that time of the war the news was very encouraging, so the guys operating the radio would say, "Don't start yelling! The war's not over, so don't be making a lot of noise and attract attention."

I think we were the only barracks with a radio—the only one I knew of, anyway—and since everyone was hungry to know the latest, someone would transcribe what we heard, and next day someone would go from barracks to barracks and read the transcription to the other POW's. That way everyone was up to date. If there was a danger that he might get caught, the guy with the transcription was instructed to eat it.

It beats the hell out of me how they got that radio, the parts, whoever it was who did it. It was already there when I arrived. It was the most secret thing in the whole camp. They would take it apart after the news and different guys would have different pieces that they hid, then after the barracks were shut down for the night they would put all the pieces back together and we'd have a radio again. The Germans never did find it. They never even looked for it because they had no idea we had it. A perfectly-kept secret

In the prison camp there was a guy from Oklahoma I liked a lot. I called him "Okie." He was in the same room I was in. One time we were talking and I said, "Okie, if and when we ever get out of here, what are you going to do when you get home? You got a job to go back to?"

He said, "No, I've always wanted to have a store."

I said, "What kind of a store?"

He said, "Oh, a store where you can sell all kinds of merchandise—you know, washers and dryers and refrigerators and stuff like that."

And I said, "Oh, like an appliance store."

"Yeah," he said, "that's it."

So I said, "You know, I've got a piece of paper here"—we didn't have much paper in camp, but I happened to have a little bit at the time—"and a pencil, so you can draw the front of the store, how you want it to look, with your name on it to identify you and what your store will sell."

He said, "Yeah, that's a good idea, Carl," so I left the pencil and paper with him.

A couple days later I saw him and asked, "Did you ever make that drawing, Okie?"

He said, "Yeah, I did, Carl."

I said, "Well let me see it." So I looked at it, and it was more or less a picture of a store, and across the top of it was a sign with the words "Electric Commodes." I said, "What the hell is an electric commode, Okie?"

He said, "Well, I wanted it to say 'electric commodities,' but I didn't have enough room to put down the whole thing."

That was the first time I'd ever heard of an electric commode, and I haven't heard of one since, though I *have* heard that in Japan they have commodes with all sorts of bells and whistles that might qualify. Maybe Okie was just ahead of his time. I have no idea if he went back and opened a store, but I hope he did.

Gives you an idea of how we yearned for an ordinary life—owning a store, building houses, being an engineer, selling insurance, fixing cars. Being a prisoner gives you a sense of appreciation you probably never had before.

PART 4 -- GOING BACK HOME

I wasn't in prison camp all that long. Five, six months at the most. February the sixth, 1945, the guards pulled everybody out of the camp—and we numbered in the thousands, six or seven, maybe more—and put us on the road. Said we'd be walking for three days or so. They divided us into groups. In the group I was in there were about sixty guys. The groups stayed together so we got to know each other, which helped when there was any kind of trouble.

The rumor was, the peace was going to be breaking out somewhere between the Russian territory and the American territory, and the Germans didn't want to give up to the Russians. Our camp was in east Germany, near Poland and the eastern front, so near that we could hear the artillery, and judging by the volume of it, which day by day got louder and louder, we could tell the Russians were advancing. So the Germans knew the Russians were going to get there before the Americans, and even though they didn't say anything, we knew that was why they had us on the road. They'd heard—we'd all heard—how brutal the Russians were. We didn't know where we were marching to, exactly, only that they wanted to get away from the Russians, to get to the American zone and surrender there. And we also knew it would take more than any three days.

Once they got us divided into groups they said, "Follow us," and away we went. We each had an over-coat and a knit hat that the Red Cross had provided, plus the blanket we got when we arrived at the camp, and that was it. We walked for several hours, until it started turning dark. Some of the older guards—a lot of them were older, because the younger soldiers were on the fronts—were assigned to carry big heavy machine guns with tripods and ammo, but the first ditch they came to they threw them away, they were so heavy.

It got colder and colder. Finally we stopped. There was snow on the ground. But the only place where we could sleep was on the ground, in the snow. Bill Henderson and I laid one blanket on the ground, pulled the other one over us, and slept the best we could. With our clothes on, of course, except for my shoes. We had walked maybe thirty kilometers, and my feet had started swelling up. They felt frozen, like my hands. It was a hard night to sleep.

Next morning they woke us up hollering, *"Raus! Raus!"* Let's get going! I could hardly get my shoes on, my feet were swollen up so bad. I finally got them on, but I couldn't lace them up. Then the guards realized that they had taken us the wrong way, east toward the Russians rather than west toward the Americans, so we had to turn around and retrace our footsteps. We joked that it was no wonder they were losing the war—the clowns couldn't tell east from west.

Eventually the swelling of my feet went down a little, enough that I could lace up my shoes.

The second night they had made arrangements with a farmer who had a big barn. They put the cattle out and put us POW's in. There was a big hay loft, but there were also animal droppings all over the floor, and there wasn't any fresh straw, so it wasn't a very comfortable place, but it was a damn sight better than lying in the snow on the ground, so we laid down and tried to sleep. That was the routine they had us follow every day: we would walk, then they would put us up for the night in one of these big barns the Germans had.

One day, not long after we'd started this march, the guards disappeared, so there were all these GI's, thousands of us, walking along the road and not a German in sight. Up and down the line guys were saying, "Let's make a break for it."

Bill said to me, "What do you think, Carl?"

I said, "Well, we sure as hell don't look like Germans, we're not dressed like Germans, and we can't speak German—I mean, even if we did get away, we're out in the country by ourselves... I think it's a trap."

So we decided not to try to escape. But some guys did. They ran off into the woods, and then we heard guns firing. So that was where the Germans were—in the woods waiting for POW's to try an escape, and then shoot them. For them, the war wasn't over till it was over. Even though it was over.

The order of the day every day was to walk. We would walk forty-five, fifty minutes, then stop and rest up for about ten minutes, then get back up and start walking again. We were fairly strong at the beginning of the march—I would guess I was about a hundred and thirty pounds, down from a hundred and sixty, but still far from infirm---but as we kept walking day after day without much food, without much water, we got weaker.

We were often hungry as hell. So hungry we could eat nails. Sometimes, when we hadn't had anything to eat for a day or two, our stomachs blew up like balloons. We obsessed over food, thought about it, dreamed about it. When we'd stop for the night, sometimes, when there was an onion field, we'd dig some up and eat them like they were apples or pears. When we passed a barley field, we'd shell some from the stalks and eat that. Just about anything we could get our hands on we'd eat. Once I saw a guy chase a pig down, cut off its tail, and eat it. That's how desperate you could get.

One of the worst things about it was we all had dysentery. We couldn't hold what little nourishment we got, so we were going downhill. You could practically see guys losing weight. But we walked anyway—that was the order of the day every day.

We had a horse-drawn wagon that followed us not far behind, and we happened to have a doctor in our group. When guys fell out and couldn't make it, we'd put them on the wagon for the doctor to take care of. He didn't have much of anything in the way of medicine, but he did the best he could. I don't think we left anybody in our group behind. Sometimes there were no horses, and when that happened some POW's would pull the wagon.

One night, instead of sleeping in a barn, we slept in a prison camp we had come upon. The camp was already over-crowded with hundreds of prisoners, prisoners of all sorts and all colors—I couldn't figure out where all they came from. We were ordered in and told we were going to be there for the night. There were barracks, but no bunks and no wood floors even, just dirt. Worse than the barns. We were warned that the prisoners there were desperate and would steal the shirts off our backs, the shoes off our feet, so to be careful. The guards allowed us to go cut down some boughs from pine trees to make a bed with if we wanted, but most of us were so tired we didn't bother and just slept on the dirt. It was god awful in that camp, so crowded, so dirty, so desperate. As it happened, no one got robbed or harmed.

But next morning Bill said, "Carl, you go and just leave me here. I can't make it any more."

I said, "What's the matter, man?"

He said, "Look. I can't touch my shoulders." He was trembling very badly. "I can't tie my shoes. I can't button my shirt. Just leave me."

I said, "I can't do that. They're gonna kill you if I leave you here." So I put his shoes on, tied them for him, buttoned his shirt up, took what little stuff he had and put it with mine, put his arm around my shoulder and said, "Grab a hold and hang on, we're going." So we took off.

For a couple of weeks he was real bad, but then, even though we weren't getting nearly enough to eat, he started getting better. After a while he was able to take care of himself pretty good. Amazing. Years later he wrote a little book, with the dedication, "To Carl Weller: without his help I never would have made it." I thought that was very nice of him.

What made it all worse in a way, and yet better, was that the countryside was so beautiful you couldn't believe it. Hills, forests of evergreens and birches, farmers' fields. It looked a lot like northern Michigan to me. Now and then we'd see deer. Made me even more homesick.

At night they'd make a big pot of soup. Instead of rutabaga they boiled up these big turnips they called kohlrabi that they had chopped up. Not the same as rutabaga, exactly, these big turnips, but no better. No meat in the soup, just water and salt and kohlrabi. But it was something to eat. Though not much, not nearly enough. We were all losing weight. For breakfast they served, if that's the word, ersatz coffee, if that's the word.

We weren't on a highway, just country roads, so we came across these farms with big barns that we slept in. On some of these farms you'd see a big mound of dirt, maybe a hundred feet long, maybe longer. The farmers grew potatoes and stored them in these mounds. They layered them—dirt, potatoes, a layer of straw, then potatoes on top of that, more dirt, more straw, and so on. So when we saw one of these mounds, we knew there were potatoes in there. Potatoes that the guards didn't want us to have.

The guards would post a soldier on each end of the mound, but sometimes they would get together, smoke a cigarette and talk. If you could get on the blind side, where they couldn't see you, you could crawl out of the barn on your belly, infantry style—I don't think that was what that training back in Texas was for, but it did finally pay off—dig into the dirt, get two or three potatoes, and put them inside your jacket, and crawl back to the barn. When we got some of those spuds to go with the kohlrabi soup, it was like a three-course meal.

There were concoctions we put together, when we could get the ingredients. We'd mix some German margarine with powdered milk and a dash of ersatz coffee, for example. When we could we'd add to that a bit of sugar, which made it a lot better. When we could add to that some cocoa, we had fudge.

For real food we had to depend on the Red Cross for food parcels. But there weren't hardly any. When we started out everyone got one parcel apiece. We didn't eat the food all at once—we wanted to make it last, to help ourselves keep going a day at a time. Everybody loved the chocolate. There were also vitamin C tablets, in a little cellophane package. A lot of guys said they didn't want them, and I said, "Anybody who doesn't want the vitamin C tablets, give them to me." They gave me their vitamin C tablets, which I ate like candy. The parcels included small packets of cigarettes, too. But they lasted for only about two weeks, something like that, and that was it.

After the war was over the Allies found those food parcels all over the place. Instead of giving all of them to the prisoners, the Germans had stored thousands of them in warehouses. Whole warehouses! Who knows, maybe they were eating them themselves. There wasn't much to eat in Germany at that time, even for the Germans.

The walk was mostly boring. After the day was over you were tired, really tired, and you had a little soup and some potato, if you could manage to steal any, and that's what you lived on. I think the farmers kind of knew what was going on, that we were stealing some of their spuds, but I don't think they really cared. I think they were actually glad, many of them. I say that because we would pass by farm houses where they would put water out for us, fresh water to drink. The guards would come along and tip the water over, just to be mean, I think. Sour grapes because they were losing the war.

The farther we went, the worse we got, physically. Some fellows had trouble with their feet—blisters, mostly. They'd fall out and get on the wagon back there and the doctor would take care of them as best he could. Like I said, everybody had the GI's—your bowels were in such bad shape you couldn't control yourself—and I mean everybody had them. The only thing the doctor could give you was charcoal. Granulated charcoal. It absorbed a lot of the water, helped a little bit.

At night you were so tired, you'd lay down for a good night's sleep, if you can call it that, but all at once you'd feel little bugs crawling up your back. Lice. Everybody had them. Body lice. Head lice. You'd look at some of the guys with big heavy heads of hair, unlike me, and you could *see* the lice crawling around in their hair. There was nothing you could do about it. Not much anyway. When you stopped for a break you could take your shirt off and go through it, killing all the lice, or so you thought, but when you put your shirt back on, zip!, you could feel them coming back at you. They robbed you of many a night's sleep.

The lice along with the GI's was... *ay yi yi yi.* You had to go to the toilet, you had no toilet paper, you had no facilities at all—you had maybe a hand full of leaves, something like that, and lice crawling all over you day and night. Those two things, the GI's and the lice, were just about unbearable, partly because you knew they weren't going away.

We were on the road three months and never took a shower. We came to the Elbe one time, and a bunch of us waded in, clothes and all. It was cold, but it felt good just to have water touching your body. Along the way we'd try to take sponge baths. You might have a piece of soap, maybe you didn't. We would try to trade with some of the guards, with some of the Germans on the farms we came across, trade cigarettes for soap. Cigarettes were like money. You could trade for all sorts of things with cigarettes—a piece of soap, a piece of bread, if you were lucky, but there wasn't much of that around.

I remember one time we came into this farmyard, and there was a chicken. She was all by herself, running around trying to stay out of our way, out of our reach, so she wouldn't get trapped. One guy had a tree limb, more like a stick, a walking stick; he threw it at that chicken and it was spinning in mid-air and damned if it didn't hit that chicken. Must have beaned her in the head, because it knocked her out. The G.I. ran over and picked the chicken up and put her inside his shirt, and I thought, "Man, if any of the Germans have seen him do that, they're gonna shoot him for sure." But they must not have seen him because he got away with it. I don't know how he ate it. Only that I didn't get any.

One time Bill and I traded something, I don't remember what, but we traded it with this kid for an egg. Just one egg. Then we wondered how we were going to eat it. We couldn't fry it or poach it, and we didn't have any water. But we agreed that maybe we could get some water and put it in a can and boil it and have a hard-boiled egg. And that's what we managed to do. When we divided it, we cut it right down the middle, and it had to be just right, both pieces *exactly* the same size. Things you never thought you'd be doing your whole life.

Now and then the guards would disappear again, trying to get some of us to try another escape. But after that first time I don't think anyone fell for it.

Towards the end of the walk, every once in a while we'd see American planes go over, P-51's mainly. They would fly low, tip their wings and do a barrel roll, which we called victory rolls, to say we're thinking of you and we're on our way. And we'd all holler and applaud and say to each other, "Oh baby, the war's gonna be over any minute now." They knew who we were, unlike when we were marching *to* the camp, because we were headed toward the Allied front. Also, they knew through our intelligence that the Germans were emptying the camps out because the Russians were coming. Since we were walking on country roads, we never saw any

German planes or tanks or anything like that, things that

would be targets for American or British planes.

After walking for three months or so, the desig-

nated leader of us POW's, a guy named Paul—don't

remember his last name—he came into the barn we were

sleeping in. We were waking up, slowly getting ready to

go out and start walking again, and Paul came in and

said, "Okay, fellas, this morning when you go out to

walk, I want you to look your best. Remember you're

American soldiers. Throw your shoulders back and try to

march in step with each other."

Bill said, "What's going on? Why do you want us

to walk like that, Paul? Where we going?"

And Paul said, "We're going home." And he

turned around and walked out. We were hollering and

crying and laughing—ecstatic, you know? Overwhelmed with happiness.

About fifteen, twenty minutes after we'd started walking again, we reached the American zone, in Fallingsbostel, I think it was. There was a bridge over a river we had to cross. The bridge had been all blown up, so the combat engineers had put a temporary bridge underneath it. Most of us prisoners continued to walk, right across the bridge, though the Germans didn't—they stayed put, threw their weapons down on the ground and threw their hands up in the air. Some of the guys went after some of the guards. I later heard that there was one guard in particular some guys went after and killed him. Big Stoop. As to how they killed him, there were different stories—bayonet, hatchet, club—but they did kill him, for a fact. But the vast majority of us didn't go after any guards; we were just so happy that we were free, we didn't want any more struggle and strife.

That was the 28th of April, 1945. We had been on the road, on foot, for three months, since April sixth. We had walked some four-hundred-and-fifty, five hundred miles. I had lost a lot of weight. Weighed about a hundred and ten by then, at most, I would guess. Maybe just a hundred. Many guys were down to ninety and even lower. We looked like the pictures of concentration camp prisoners you've seen, skin and bones. I learned later that thirteen hundred or so men died on that march. Well over ten percent of the men who started. It became known as the German Death March, or just The March, like the one over in the Pacific Theater—Bataan.

On the other side of the river was like a barracks where the Germans had been ensconced and where we were to stay. They wouldn't give us anything to eat, even though were a very skinny lot—emaciated, down to a hundred pounds and even lower, like I said—but they didn't want us getting sick. "Your stomachs may not be handle to handle the food we've got, they said. "We don't know." We were disappointed, to put it mildly, but they had a point. And we did have a consolation prize: there were bunk beds in the barracks, something we hadn't seen in a long time. They assigned us beds and we fell into them right away, we were so tired.

It was maybe three or four o'clock in the morning when some guy came along and started shaking my bed. I woke up and said, "What the hell do you want?"

He said, "Are you Carl Weller?"

I said, "Yes I am,"

He said, "You're on KP in half an hour."

I said, "What! KP in half an hour! We just got here and a few hours sleep and I'm on KP!"

He said, "Well you can go talk to the cook about it if you want. I'm just giving you the message."

So I put some clothes on and walked over to the kitchen and said to the cook, "I don't know what the hell is going on here, but I'm going to go back to bed. I'm not going to do KP."

He said, "Don't worry about that. Someone is probably playing a joke on you."

On my way back to the barracks I passed by a room that was full of canned food, so I unbuttoned my shirt and started stuffing it with cans of peaches and pine-apple and such and took them back to the barracks with me, so we could have something to eat. I knew the food might make us sick, but I was willing to risk it—hell, we were hungry!—so I took matters into my own hands, literally. And we ate all that canned fruit without any ill effects, I'm happy to say.

They said they were going to bring in C-54 airplanes to pick us up and take us to Camp Lucky Strike near Le Havre, in Normandy, where we'd ship out for home. There were a bunch of camps in that area named after cigarette brands: Old Gold, Chesterfield, Philip Morris, Pall Mall, and Lucky Strike. Smoking wasn't frowned on in those days. In fact, it was sort of the thing to do. These camps had been set up after the invasion of Normandy and were used as staging areas for incoming troops. Now, at the war's end, they were used as staging areas for troops going back home.

Well, we waited and waited and waited. Days went by and nothing happened. All that time the guys running the camp stayed real careful about what they would let us eat—really bland stuff that they considered safe, like milk and potatoes, because they were afraid that most foods could mess up our stomachs and they weren't sure which ones.

I collected a lot of souvenirs, went out and picked up officers' uniforms, pistols, daggers, whatever. But being stuck in that camp like that really got to us. It was like now we were in an *American* prison camp.

While we were waiting, and waiting and waiting and waiting, General Eisenhower was on his way to somewhere or other, I forget where now, and he stopped at this camp with all these POW's, thousands of us, and he said, "Who are all those men out there?"

The officers in charge said, "They're POW's, sir."

And he said, "What the hell are they doing there?"

They said, "Well, we're waiting for C-54's to come in and fly them out, take them to Camp Lucky Strike."

He said, "How long have they been here?"

They said, "A couple of weeks."

Eisenhower said, "When I've taken care of my business, I'm coming back this way, tomorrow, and I want all these people to be gone."

They said, "Yes sir!" And believe me, they jumped to it. But even so, they couldn't ship everyone out all at once—there were way too many of us—so there was still a lot of waiting yet for a lot of soldiers.

While we were all waiting I got reacquainted with a man named Jack Stiddam, a guy from Lexington, Kentucky. He and I were in a couple of classes together back at Lowry, when we were learning how to take machine guns apart and put them back together, all that kind of stuff, and we always had a good time. So we buddied up, and Jack said to me one day, "You know, Carl, these guys are doing their best, but they've got their hands full. The C-54's are gonna come, no doubt, but who knows when? Why don't we just get the hell out of here? Maybe we can find Camp Lucky Strike by ourselves."

The war wasn't officially quite over yet—that was the next day, but we didn't know it would be the next day. Even so, I said, "Good idea." I hated to leave those souvenirs behind, but we were tired of being tied up in this camp. So we walked out of the gate.

The guard at the gate said, "Hey, where you guys going?"

We said, "We're going home."

He said, "Whatta you mean, you're going home?"

We said, "We getting tired of waiting around here. We don't think they're ever going to take care of us, so we're gonna find our way home."

And he said, "Hey, good idea."

We said, "We gotta get to Camp Lucky Strike. We know that."

He said, "I'll tell you what. There are Army trucks going back and forth on this road all the time. Stick your thumb out and get a ride. Tell them you want to go to the airport."

We went out on the road and the first truck that came by, the driver stopped and said, "Where you guys going?"

We said, "We want to go to Camp Lucky Strike,"

He said, "You're a long ways from Camp Lucky Strike. But there's a little airfield down the road—I'll drop you off there." So he did.

There was a C-54 on the runway and they were revving up the engines. This major came up to me and said, "Who are you?"

I said, "We're both ex-prisoners of war. We're trying to get to Camp Lucky Strike."

And he said, "Well, I've got this plane on the runway. We're not going to Camp Lucky Strike, but I'll be glad to give you a ride to Versailles. Do you have any I.D.? Dog tags? Papers?"

I said, "No, we don't."

He said, "God, you've gotta have I.D. I don't know who you are. Tell you what. Go to the little town down the road—it's only a couple of miles—and see the provost marshal there. Get him to testify you're Americans, get it down on paper, signed and certified, and I can take you. I'll hold the plane for you, but you gotta hurry." We said thanks and went out the gate.

There were some guards there talking to a couple of girls. There were two bicycles leaning against the fence—they belonged to the girls, presumably. We grabbed the bicycles to ride to the town and said, "Don't worry. We're gonna bring your bicycles right back."

We rode into the town and went to the provost marshal. He asked us some questions about stuff we should know—serial numbers, outfits, POW experience, that sort of thing. He was satisfied and gave us a piece of paper that said we were Americans. We rode back to the camp and dropped the bicycles off. We didn't know where the girls were—they were gone. The guards were gone too. We went back to the major and he put us on the C-54 and it took off. There were no seats on it, so we just sat on the bottom of the fuselage. Turned out that this was not U.S. Army. It was A.T.C., Air Transport Command, and what they did was deliver stuff. And now they were delivering us.

After a while we landed on an airfield near Versailles. We got off the plane and a fellow said, "Where the hell did you guys come from?" We told him we came from Fallingsbostel, and he said, "I want you to go out to the middle of this field"—it was like a baseball diamond—"take all your clothes off and put them on the ground beside you." So we did. Wound up standing in the middle of this field butt naked. They made a pile of our clothes, poured gasoline on it and lit it. They had long sticks with bags of DDT on them, and they beat us on the head and all over with these bags, because we had lice so bad.

Then they led us inside to a shower room, gave us soap, wash cloths, and towels. Luxury items. They didn't have to tell us what to do. We must have stayed in that shower forty, fifty minutes, it felt so good to wash off three months of dirt. More than three months, actually—we were pretty dirty when we left the Stalag. To feel all clean again was like a renewal, a new lease on life.

Finally we came out and they gave us fresh uniforms. Then we took a little nap. When we woke up, one of the guys in the barracks we were in said, "You know, the war is officially over. VE Day—Victory in Europe Day. The French people are having a wonderful time, and they're gonna have a big party in Versailles tonight—would you guys like to go along with us?"

I said, "Oh, I think we can do that."

So that night they took us to the town of Vers-

ailles, and the French people were out on the streets

celebrating, carrying torches, singing songs, drinking

champagne and cognac and anything else they could get

their hands on. It was one big party, a rip-roaring event.

They offered me champagne, *and* wine and cognac, and

unfortunately I accepted their offers. All of them. Got

sicker than heck because my body just wasn't used to

alcohol.

We got up the next day and went back to town

and got a bus to a passenger train and went to Paris. We

went straight to the Red Cross—God bless the Red

Cross!—and they gave us cigarettes, they gave us money,

they gave us candy, they gave us meal tickets so we

could go to restaurants, and they gave us tickets to use at

hotels. (I probably shouldn't be telling this because we

were actually AWOL, but then we didn't belong to any

outfit, we were just ex-POW's, and I assume I'm safe these many years later—after all, there must be a statute of limitations for AWOL's.) So we stayed there for several days enjoying just being free, being able to walk around and eat and drink as we pleased. We got a haircut, got our shoes shined, got all spiffed up as if for a Saturday night, which every day felt like. A holiday.

Then we got on a train that went to Camp Lucky Strike. We were sitting on the train waiting for it to go and a couple of MP's got on board looking around. One of them looked at us and said, "Are there any ex POW's on this train?"

I looked at Jack and he looked at me. We didn't know what they wanted—for all we knew, to send us back to the American camp in Fallingsbostel—so we played it safe and said, "No, I don't think so."

And he said, "Well, if you see any of them, tell them they don't have to go. They can stay here as long as they want—we won't bother them."

We said, "Well, thanks." We debated a little bit. Paris was great, but we were homesick, wanted to go home. So we stayed on the train and went to Camp Lucky Strike because that was where the boats were loading up the troops and taking them back to the States.

Camp Lucky Strike was even bigger than Fallingsbostel. Thousands and thousands of tents. We looked for the guys we had left behind there, but they still hadn't arrived. A couple days later they showed up. They were surprised to see us. That's about the way it was—guys would separate for all sorts of reasons, then occasionally some of us would run back into each other. A very arbitrary, hit-or-miss affair, life in the Service in a war.

I wondered if my pilot, Bob Felgar, was there. I hadn't seen him since we had the plane shot out from under us. So I went from tent to tent asking people if anybody had seen him. Finally, after two days, a guy said, "Yeah, I saw him yesterday." He told us where Bob was and we went over there and sure enough he was there.

We had a good reunion. He was in pretty good shape, actually, considering. That was when I found out what all happened to him, the blow to his head, his fingers getting blown off, coming to in a spin that pinned him in, how the big explosion blew him out of the plane at three thousand feet and how he managed to pull the rip cord. He hit the ground pretty hard, and the Germans took him right away, but he was alive. Even safe, in a sense. It was a miracle. We agreed that it was a miracle that any of us survived.

Then he said, "You know, Carl, the thing about me is my back. I can't reach it, and I've got these little pieces of aluminum stuck in it. Maybe you can pull them out for me." So I told him to take his tee shirt off, and I pulled out all these little pieces of aluminum that were stuck in his back, *still* there months after we had been hit.

I was in Camp Lucky Strike about a week. Not too long. The camp was a lot nicer than Fallingsbostel. We had enough to eat—we were eating anything we wanted to now—and compared to prison camp, it was fine dining. And yeah, we were in tents, but we had beds to sleep on—cots, actually, but with sheets and blankets and pillows, everything we needed to get a good night's sleep.

Le Havre was a port. We all went home by boat. Jack Stiddam didn't get on the same ship as I did. The ship I got on, I don't remember the name of. All the ships were what they called Liberty Ships. It wasn't an ocean liner, I can tell you that. So, after having traveled about four hundred-and-fifty, five hundred miles on foot, and what?—a couple of hundred miles by plane and train?—we were going to sail thirty-five hundred miles by water. Quite a journey, all told.

On the boat back home there was a lot of gambling going on. We had gotten back pay. It was quite a bit, actually. Eight months, plus ten percent hazard pay for all the missions we flew, and that continued while we were in prison camp, until we got back home. So there were a lot of games going on. I didn't gamble myself. Oh, once in a while I played a little bit, but never for more than a couple dollars. Some of the guys were card sharks—they were good—and a lot of money changed hands. But there weren't any fights, none that I knew of anyway. We were all too happy to fight, happy to be on our way home.

The voyage to New York was uneventful, thank God. As far as I was concerned, I'd had enough events to last a lifetime.

When we got back to the States I was in pretty good shape. A lot better than I was at the end of the march. Still a little underweight, but I didn't have any-thing wrong with me physically—no injuries, no disease. Getting back, some of the guys were a little nervous, as we said then—post traumatic syndrome they call it now, or something like that—but if I had it, it was a very mild case.

They sent us to Florida. A hotel in Miami. I think this was in July. It was real hot weather, and there was no air conditioning in those days. I remember you'd get up and take a shower, put your uniform on, and go to this restaurant a couple of blocks away for breakfast, and by the time you got there you were wringing wet again, it was so hot and humid. But it was great to be in a place where you didn't have to do anything, any marching or stuff like that. Just get lazy, eat good food, enjoy the sunshine—it was wonderful. Felt good to be alive.

I thought that the minute we got back to the States I would be discharged from the Army, but in Florida they told me I didn't have enough points yet. This was a new one on me.

I said, "What are you talking about?"

They said, "Well, you need so many points to be discharged. You haven't been in long enough to get enough." I thought that was the most ridiculous thing I'd ever heard of. "But," they said, "you *can* go anywhere you want. So where do you want to go?"

I said, "How about Selfridge?" because that was in Michigan, the closest base to home.

They said, "No, there are no openings there. But anywhere *else* you want to go."

I said, "Okay, how about Chicago?" which was the next closest place to home.

And they said, "Well, there's nothing there either. But anywhere you want to go other than those two."

By this time I figured they meant as long as it was nowhere near home. Unless this whole thing was a comedy routine. So I said, "I'll tell you what. I love Denver. I was there during training. Just send me back there." And whatta you know?—they did!

They gave me this job where I sat at a desk in a hotel-like place, in a railroad terminal. They would bring me papers for maybe two hundred men who were going somewhere on a train, and these papers were their records. All I had to do was give the men their papers. They'd sign a form stating that I had given their papers to them, and that was it. Some days no one went through there. When I was done I'd have the rest of the day to myself. That was a really great assignment.

There was a little restaurant connected to the office I was in that had a nice soda bar and some beautiful girls there, young women who would make me a big malted milk with a lot of ice cream in it. Every day they would make me one. I hadn't had a malt in a long long time, you know. And seen beautiful American girls. It was great. Wonderful. Heaven.

Another thing about Denver—and the whole country, actually—you could go out on the road, stick your thumb out, and the first car that came by would stop and pick you up and take you where you wanted to go, or as close to it as possible. People there just loved the

GI's, it seemed to me. They had so much respect for us.

Several of us liked to go out in the mountains and

just relax. There was this little bar we liked to go to

called the Swing Inn, so we'd stop there and have a beer.

We got to know quite a few of the people around there

because we'd go there every chance we got. Once a

buddy and I overstayed our visit there, and it started to

get dark. We had to get back to town, and the road was

just a little two-lane job. We stuck our thumb out and

this fellow in a Model A Ford pickup truck stopped and

asked where we wanted to go. We said Denver, and he

said, "Yeah, I'll take you. Get in." Well, that was a ride

I'll never *ever* forget. That guy should have been a pur-

suit pilot. He went down that road lickety-split,

careening and sliding around curves, flooring it on

straightaways. When he dropped us off I was glad to get

back on the ground again. But I have to say, that boy should have been racing stock cars. Or running moonshine.

I was in Denver three or four months. It was this point thing again. I had to stay there to build up enough points to get out of the Service. I finally did and they sent me to Chicago. The Army made a film there about some of our missions and about getting shot down. They wanted to know exactly what happened on our last mission. Felgar didn't want to talk about it, Benitez couldn't talk about since he had died, so they turned to me and said, "Okay, Carl, you're going to have to do it." They sat me down in a chair, put a spotlight on me, and there was a lady there who filmed the interview. It was quite an interview—I would say about an hour and a half long.

It was sort of like the interrogation when you finished a mission, only this one was much delayed, since we didn't have an interrogation after being shot down, of course. But this one was more detailed—there was more to talk about—because on some of our missions nothing unusual or dramatic really happened: we went, we dropped our bombs, we returned, simple as that. So when we got all done with this interview in Chicago, I asked if I could have a copy of it. The woman said it would go to the Library of Congress and I could get a copy from them. Years later my daughter Wendy wrote them asking for a copy but never heard anything back. I'm sure they have the tape, but I don't think they'll give us a copy of it. I don't know why I don't think so, and I don't know why they won't, but it's all pretty disappointing. It was an interesting interview because most of what happened was fresh in my mind then.

They gave me a physical and my discharge papers. I had a bus pass to get home to Detroit, and I had a few dollars in my pocket, not a lot. I went to the bus station and bought a ticket to Detroit, but the bus was going to be leaving later in the evening, so I had to wait a while. There was a bar across the street, and I thought I'd go over and have a beer, just sit and relax. I was all by myself. I went in the bar and ordered a shell of beer and that was the last thing I remembered.

I woke up next day in a bed in the Salvation Army building. My money was gone, my wallet, my ticket, everything. I couldn't believe it. I had taken maybe one sip of that beer and *bam!* I was out like a light. I don't know what it was exactly that they gave me, but it was powerful. So not everyone was nice to the GI's. But the people at the Salvation Army were—they helped me get a ticket to go home, so I finally made it to Detroit.

I took a cab from the bus station to the house. My mother knew I was coming—I had wired her. Many hugs and kisses and tears. Then I said, "Where's Dad?"

She said, "Where he usually is. At the Corner Bar."

So I went to the bar. He said, "Welcome home, son. Have a seat. Have a beer." I sat down with him and we had a couple of beers together. First time. Though he didn't say much—he was not the demonstrative type—I could tell he was really glad to see me. Everybody there was glad to see me. And at last I felt I was really back home.

But even so I thought about that old German soldier—*"Alles ist kaputt"*—and about the kid Benitez going down in flames on his first mission. I still do. So the war is over, has been over for almost seventy years, but for me it has never been entirely over. Some things you just don't get over, and maybe it's just as well—it means that some things really matter, that's why you still care.

Here's a postscript. I have been asked if I have any bitterness over the war and my ordeal in it. I did. For a long time I wouldn't talk about it, and I drank too much—what they call self-medication, these days—but eventually I decided to focus on my blessings. I had a good life—a good marriage, kids, business, friends—and in time the bitterness and anger worked their way out. If you harbor grudges and bitterness, you turn sour, and everyone knows that sweet milk is a whole lot better than sour. So I opted for sweet.

And here's a post-postscript. I was in Germany recently, spent a couple of weeks with a German family who knew of my war record there. They couldn't have been nicer, more hospitable. We got along great, had a wonderful time. Soon before I left we were having dinner in a restaurant and talked a little about the war among other things. A young man from a nearby table was leaving and stopped at our table. He looked at me and said—and this was in all sincerity, without a trace of sarcasm—he said, "I overheard you talking about your service in the war. I want to thank you for what you did for Germany." I've gotta tell you, I *never* expected to hear *that* from a German. It felt good.

ABOUT THE AUTHOR

After the war Carl Weller worked as a railroad switchman for several years, then worked for several more as a factory rep selling appliances, radios and TV's (which were brand new at the time). He married and had three kids. He and his wife Mickey bought and restored a Victorian house in Ypsilanti, Michigan, then bought an old (1845) flour mill in Saline, Michigan, plus a building behind it that Henry Ford had built to extract oil from soy beans for manufacturing plastic. Both buildings not only had no plumbing or electricity, they were derelict. Carl and his wife and their children restored and renovated them, turning them first into an antique mall, then into a catering business that grew to the point that they could host three parties at one time, indoors *and* outdoors. Carl is now retired and living in Saline, enjoying the fruits of his labors.

ABOUT THE EDITOR

Jeff Duncan is a retired Professor of English at Eastern Michigan University. He has published numerous articles and several books of various sorts—literary criticism, textbook, memoir, poetry. As Playwright in Residence at Wild Swan Theater in Ann Arbor for twenty-five years, he has had over thirty plays produced in many venues all around Michigan and adjoining states.